Occultism in America is exploding at a rate most of us would have thought unbelievable a few years ago. The scene today can't be denied . . . or ignored. From Satan worship to syndicated columns on astrology, we're in the Age of the Occult. The path from drugs to devil worship has been freewheeling and fast travelled.

Housewives, professional people, businessmen and students are caught in the surge of the supernatural. What was formerly taboo is now "with it". What's it all about?

In this well-documented book Gary penetrates through the maze of fraud and fantasy in the occult. He reveals the supernatural world in its proper perspective and offers the solution for those who are searching for true spiritual dimension.

I believe he is one of the outstanding youth leaders in the country today. His investigations into the dangers of the spirit world are desperately needed.

HAL LINDSEY

The Fortune Sellers

by Gary Wilburn

A Division of G/L Publications
Glendale, California, U.S.A.

Scripture quoted from *New American Standard Bible.* © The Lockman
Foundation, 1971. Used by permission.

© Copyright 1972 by G/L Publications
All rights reserved
Printed in U.S.A.

Published by
Regal Books Division, G/L Publications
Glendale, California 91209, U.S.A.

Library of Congress Catalog Card No. 73-190509
ISBN 0-8307-0151-6

Dedicated to
my wife Beverly
whom I love

Contents

Preface

The word *occult* by definition means those things hidden or secret. In light of the recent popularity of these magical arts, a new name for them might be in order.

In trying to categorize the various forms of occult practice today, I have attempted the impossible. As soon as one particular deviation is popularized, another crops up. In addition to this there is so much interblending of occult practice as will be described in this book:

Chapters 1, 2 and 3 are introductory;

Chapters 4, 5 and 6 deal with the art of *mantic* or "fortune-telling" as it is commonly called;

Chapters 7, 8 and 9 consider *magic,* both "black" and "white";

Chapters 10 and 11 are concerned with *spiritualism,* the third main division of the occult;

Chapter 12 is a summation of the foregoing chapters.

I would like to thank the many writers and scholars whose research I have incorporated herein. I am only sorry that my conclusions are oftentimes different than theirs. A word of thanks, also, to Mr. Paul Hetrick, my dear friend who assisted in the final editing of this manuscript.

> *"It's in the very trickery that it pleases me. But show me how the trick is done, and I have lost my interest therein."*
>
> Seneca the Younger
> *45th Epistle to Lucilius*

CHAPTER 1

Beyond the Visible World

Man lives on a planet that is concrete and visible. His personality and soul are housed within a body that is physical, touchable, knowable and seeable. He eats food that he first regards with his eyes and smells with his nose. He sleeps on a bed that is either soft or hard to the touch.

Man's world is limited by its physical qualities and knowable traits.

Or is it?

What has always made man a unique specimen of physical life is his belief in, and search for, something beyond the visible world in which he lives. He dreams and has ideas. He investigates the realms which are outside of his sense perception.

He is aware of a Being or beings separate from himself who cavort and command attention of those who inhabit the earth.

He has a profound interest in the stars, in witches, in magic. He wonders if spirits who have departed have not really departed. He yearns to understand and comprehend what exists—if anything —beyond the curtain of physical death. He wants to know his future, and so he turns to tea leaves, cards, crystal balls and his own palm.

Man is a seeker.

Though often he does not fully understand what it is he seeks, an inner drive compels him to continue his quest.

Being the pragmatist he is, he reasons that if spirits are real, they will prove it to him.

And to do this, they'll undoubtedly perform supernatural feats—like causing objects to float in the air, making eerie sounds and rapping on tables.

So reasoned the two brothers from Buffalo, New York, Ira Eratus and William Henry Davenport. They had to—spiritism was their business.

A big business indeed. From America to the British Isles, the brothers repeatedly asked to be bound and tied in wooden wardrobe cabinets. Thus secured, they would produce ghostly music on guitars, bells and tambourines while causing numerous objects to jump out of their cabinet. Their performances were always in the dark (as were most of their spectators!).

The posters billed them as "mediums" even though professional magicians viewed them much differently. Dr. T. L. Nichols, an early biographer

2

of the Davenports, reported that as boys the brothers would sometimes fly over the heads of their family and friends. Once their little sister joined them to make an eerie aerial trio. The "flying" was always done in the dark and the only proof of its occurrence would be that when people reached up, they could touch the brothers' shoes and clothing above their heads. Strangely enough, in their hundreds of public seances, the boys were always earthbound. Only their bells and guitars flew through the air.

But alas, so did their integrity.

Like the time some college students ignited matches during one of their performances only to reveal the boys, with their arms free, gleefully waving their instruments above their heads. But despite the confessions of stage crewmen and accusations by other magicians and scientists, people kept coming to be fooled. And fooled they were—throughout most of the English-speaking world.

The "spirit cabinet" trick has been duplicated by hundreds of magicians and to this day continues to mystify audiences. A hint of speculation would conclude that the main reason for its unusual popularity during the last century was an uncanny interest in the unknown, especially in the possibility of life after death.

And people today are no less interested.

The deception

These are the tricks of the trade: magic cabinets, straitjackets, chains, black art boxes, mirrors, disappearing objects and people and their reappearance. The art of magic is the art of deception. The hand is seldom quicker than the eye; the hand merely deceives the eye. In hundreds of performances, I have seen audiences of all ages stare spellbound as I passed a solid hoop around a girl floating in mid-air or escape within seconds from a mailsack inside a locked packing trunk. But this is the work of a magician, not a medium.

It's just as easy to be fooled by spiritist impostors. And more often than not, that's exactly what takes place. I am in no way ruling out the possibility of real spirit contact through mediums. It does happen. But beware of the phony!

You can usually spot a faker if what you thought would happen during the seance actually does happen. Tables "floating" off the floor, strange "rappings" on the table, clouds of smoke and eerie music are usually dead giveaways. If a cold gust of air seems to come from the ceiling and weird "2001: Space Odyssey" music is brought forth from the draperies, the best thing you can do is to ask for a cash refund.

Dimly-lit rooms and hand touching under the table are ultra-suspicious. Often a faker will ask the people on his right and left to hold each of his hands and put one of their feet on each of his. It takes little time, however, for a pro to move his or her hands and feet so that the people on each side are holding another hand and stepping on a different foot. A free hand and foot can work miracles. Presto—a pseudo-seance!

If a seance looks like something you've seen in

the movies, it's probably produced the same way—by special effects!

The Hebrew word used to describe a witch is "Ob." The word originally described the sound of a voice spoken into an empty wineskin. The same effect today could be achieved by speaking into an empty barrel. It was often a mysteriously hollow sound like this that was heard during the seances of long ago—one of the reasons being that such sittings often took place in mountain caves. These deep, echoing tones are easy sounds for an accomplished ventriloquist to produce. Whenever such a weird groan is heard during a controlled seance, you can be pretty sure that it's not a sick ghost. Real spirit contact, as we will see in a subsequent chapter, is almost always made through a medium in a trance-like stupor. The spirit's words will come through the lips of the medium, not through the loudspeaker in the ceiling.

The great escape artist

Erik Weisz was first drawn to spiritism because of his ambitious quest for truth as well as his interest in his profession. In fact, Weisz, better known as "the great Houdini," was interested to such a degree that the later years of his life were spent in discrediting the sham and trickery of his contemporaries. Many of his public performances would be divided into three segments: magic, escapes, and revelations of spiritist trickery.

Houdini's story still remains an enigma in the annals of spiritism.

In an earnest attempt to seek out any bit of truth in spiritism, Houdini had visited and interviewed professional "mediums" throughout the world. He claimed to have found not one genuine spiritist.

Houdini would challenge mediums again and again with enormous money offers, but no one would take on the master. Time after time, he would duplicate exactly the seances of the impostors to such a real and believable degree that people would often be shocked and upset when he exposed all of the gimmicks and devices used in his demonstrations.

Skeptics left happily; believers left disillusioned.

Not everyone was convinced, however. Sir Arthur Conan Doyle, creator of the fictional detective Sherlock Holmes, was equally outspoken in his affirmative belief in mediums and spirit communication. Outside of writing, his life was dedicated to furthering the cause of spiritism. A number of years and many debates later, both Doyle and Houdini held their ground in opposite corners. Doyle would tell of a real seance and Houdini would duplicate it. Doyle would then credit Houdini with a latent gift for mediumship and Houdini would laugh it off. So went the cycle until Houdini's death on October 31, 1926—Halloween!

Prior to his illness, Houdini and his wife had arranged a code whereby they would try to communicate with each other after one of them had died. The code was invented by them and guarded with maximum protection because of its use in their mind-reading acts. No other human being knew the code, nor was it ever written down for fear of detection. Houdini agreed to do anything possible to get in touch with his wife after his death using only the code.

Shortly after her husband's death, Beatrice offered $10,000 to any medium who could communicate the "Houdini Code."

Many would-be spiritists took her up on the challenge, yet after a barrage of supposed "visions" and "messages" from her husband, she withdrew the offer two years later. None of them had even faintly resembled the agreed-upon code.

The case was closed. There had been no actual communication with the dead Houdini.

Not until Reverend Arthur Ford came on the scene. Rev. Ford, a Disciples of Christ minister, was reported to have received a message from Houdini's mother during a New York seance. The message had come through a "control" spirit by the name of Fletcher (the spirit of a French-Canadian boyhood friend of Houdini who had died in his twenties). The message contained the word "forgive," a long-awaited thought of reassurance to Houdini's wife, who verified the message as being authentically based upon their code.

Less than a year later, Ford again went into a trance during which Fletcher, speaking through Ford, gave a message from Harry Houdini himself. The "dead" Houdini supposedly explained the ten-word code and asked that a meeting be arranged with his wife. According to Ford's autobiography, *Nothing So Strange*, Houdini and his wife communicated through the revealed code. The story broke like thunder the silence of supernatural activity.

Verified by an editor of *Scientific American,* who had attended each session with Ford and Mrs. Houdini, the publicity spread to two continents overnight.

Houdini was alive!

The apparent contact made with Houdini through Ford's "control" spirit, Fletcher, was taken by many to be conclusive proof of spirit communication. Professionals had witnessed it, and Mrs. Houdini herself wrote a personal note verifying everything that had happened as being true.

Yet something caused her to change her mind. Upon learning of the wildfire publicity of the seances, she immediately withdrew her endorsement of Arthur Ford and denied the documented story published in *Scientific American.*[1]

There is not, of course, sufficient evidence to prove the validity of the Houdini seances. On the other hand, Mrs. Houdini's verbal renunciation is not satisfactory proof that they were a hoax.

It does make you wonder, doesn't it?

It is estimated that today there are over 70 million people who adhere to spiritism around the world. Are these people merely suffering from a delusion—the delusion of actually being able to communicate with the departed spirits—or is there truth and validity in what they claim?

Could there be something beyond the grave, an existence for the soul and a possibility of communication with those still living? Are there forces in heaven and earth which we have never dreamed of in our philosophies? And if so are these forces good —or evil?

Come with me sometime to the Magic Castle, a private club for professional magicians in Hollywood, California, where each year a traditional seance is held. The purpose? To make contact with the late Houdini.[2]

Footnotes for Chapter 1

1. John Stevens Kerr, *The Mystery and Magic of the Occult* (Philadelphia: Fortress Press, 1971), pp. 94-96.

2. The famed agnostic, Clarence Darrow, promised Detroit businessman Claude Noble that if he found an afterlife he would manifest it on the anniversary of his death. Like the celebrated Houdini's seances, Mr. Noble's attempted communications with Darrow failed repeatedly. Even recital of the Lord's Prayer could not aid in producing the promised "violent vibration of Noble's arm." (J. K. Van Baalen, *The Chaos of the Cults.* Grand Rapids: Eerdmans, 1962, p. 52.)

PART ONE
MYSTERY

"Our Father, which wert in heaven . . ."

Satanist Prayer

CHAPTER 2

Ouija-Bored?

Her hands quivering for fear of what she might find, her mind racing a thousand times faster than the words she heard coming from the next room, Rosemary squirms through the small, secret passageway into the long hallway leading to the celebration. Bold in her search for the truth, yet afraid of its imminent terror, she enters the main room. The merriment of the songs and champagne halts as she feels the power of darkness in which seems to be a thousand eyes—all focused on her presence.

She makes her way quickly to the corner where, covered with black silk and adorned with a black cross, lies her baby. Hoping against hope, she raises the silken shroud—then covering her face in horror she jerks her fists to the ceiling and screams, "Oh God! Oh God! Oh God! Oh God! Oh God!" But Roman Castevet, her neighbor and the head witch, thunders back, "God is dead! God is dead, and Satan lives! The year is One, the first year of our lord! The year is One and God is done!"

The fear of actress Mia Farrow in the film "Rosemary's Baby" is approached only by that of those leaving the theatre. A child of Satan, born to a human mother, fulfilling the anticipation of his followers, born on Christmas day! Could such a thing really be? Could there be any truth in magic spells, boiling cauldrons, black cats and voodoo dolls? Is man really his own worst enemy?

And so it goes—not only in Greenwich Village and Haight-Ashbury, but from the Sta-Prest offices of New York to the Disneyland business suites of Southern California.

Crystal balls, Tarot cards, Ouija boards and astrological horoscopes preoccupy the consciences of thousands of religious as well as non-religious people. Games such as "Clairvoyant," "Horoscope," "Mystic Eye," "Kabala," and "Voodoo" provide more than pastimes for many who would declare themselves to be educated, enlightened and sophisticated citizens of twentieth-century America.

As civilization progresses at phenomenal speed, our technological advances and sociological superiority fail to fill the void of the supernatural. Something seems to be missing.

The recipe of the witches in Shakespeare's *Macbeth* seems charmingly simple when compared to real life. Richard Cavendish, in his book *The Black Arts*, mentions such "sacred objects" in use today as candles made of human fat, the head of a black cat fed on human flesh, a bat drowned in blood, horns of a goat that has copulated with a young girl and the skull of a parricide.[1]

Nearly every college or university, we are told by numerous television documentaries, can boast its own witch. Sybil Leek, the millionairess witch, estimates that there are more than 400 witch covens in the United States today compared with only 280 just five years ago. "Almost a thousand people tell me each week they want to be witches," says Miss Leek.[2] Not an unbelievable statement, considering the estimate of Timothy Green Beckley, publisher of *ESP* magazine, that there are at least 5,000 witches in New York and perhaps twice that many in Los Angeles.

Witches, it seems, are organizing and joining the protest parade. Lewis Martello, author of the book *The Weird Way of Witchcraft*, recently assisted New York City sorceresses in drawing up a "manifesto" demanding that civil rights legislation be extended to protect witchcraft as a formal religion and urging descendants of witches executed in Salem nearly 300 years ago to sue the Massachusetts city for $100 million in "reparations".[3]

Teilhard de Chardin, the French paleontologist who is much read on the nation's campuses today, has partially diagnosed the problem, "In the modern world with interplanetary rockets a reality, only the fantastic is likely to be true on the cosmic level.[4]

Growth of the occult

Nearly every national magazine in America has recently published articles dealing with the occult. *Life* magazine was quick to interpret the trend in a grandiose report on modern witchcraft, English version, with some alluring photos of a coven in action—first in the grand outdoors dancing around a fire, and then in the grand indoors, naked, making sinister gestures with knives at a wall adorned with cabalistic signs and symbols.

Occult sales in the past three years have more than doubled, and over two-thirds of the nation's 1,750 newspapers currently carry daily horoscope advice.[5] Tarot cards are being marketed *en masse* by several publishing companies, while "tannis root," "Satan powder" and various herbs, incense, candles and love potions are available from one's local witch store.

Most popular and highly advertised among the volumes of available occult material is the attractive publication, *Man, Myth and Magic*. "The most unusual magazine ever published," claims its editor, Richard Cavendish,[6] is a seven-volume encyclopedia of the unknown which covers every conceivable subject of mundane curiosity from "Aberdeen Witches" to "Zurvan." The youth market is proving to be a prime target for this type of publication.

"An immense amount of potentially harmful occult material is now available—to the unsuspecting public," says Dr. Charles Wahl, a professor at U.C.L.A.'s Neuro Psychiatric Institute. "We have no control over it."[7]

Esquire magazine recently published a 23-page report on the "California Evil" wherein Princess Leda (an acid goddess who used to perform nightly at Hollywood's ex-Climax club) was interviewed shortly after having supposedly copulated with a black swan.[8] The Princess Leda Amun Ra, as she would have herself believed, would regularly dance covered only with black swan feathers which she holds to be sacred along with the feathers and blood of a recently sacrificed peacock. In addition to believing herself to be a reincarnation of Amun Ra, the sun god of Thebes, she was/is also (a la reincarnation) an Atlantis high priest, as well as Sarah Bernhardt and Nephtys (who else but the sister of Isis and Osiris)!

The same magazine also interviewed Satan worshipers, mescaline freaks, the Zodiac killer and Neke Carson—a 23-year-old inventor who believes that "the Second Coming has already come. Only J.C. didn't show up; Satan did."[9] Satan, it appears to some, is alive and living well in the Hollywood hills directing an international league of people called the "Devilmen" who have let the devil into them and work for him.

Satan worship

The worship of Satan is certainly not new. During the past few years, though, Satanism has erected its ugly head in many parts of the United States, perhaps the main area being San Francisco. Anton La Vey, for the past fifteen years a practicing sorcerer, established the first "Satan Church" several

17

years ago with the doctrinal position that "we believe in the pleasures of the flesh, living to the hilt, enjoying all there is to be enjoyed on earth."[10] Certainly this enjoyment would not be complete without a new version of the insidious black mass, the baptism of his own daughter [11] and the performance of a Satanist wedding.[12]

Far from being the rejects of society, La Vey disciples are reported to include such personalities as an IBM engineer, several university professors of anthropology and members of the police force, the state government, medicine, the ministry and the bar. La Vey recently ordained fifteen priests and priestesses of his own, and the group boasts a Satanist bible as well as the possibility of a Black Mass LP record forthcoming.

Though the idea may seem bizarre and extreme, many similar churches are being established each month throughout the world. For example, the occult church in Paris with the name "We Serve the Prince of This World" and its sister churches in Basel, Berne and Rome. [13]

Don't laugh until you take a second look at the "family" of followers around the country who looked to Charles Manson as their "messiah." More frightening than the attraction of certain youth to the person of Manson is the fact that thousands were attracted by his debased philosophy of life. A national cult has been formed due to the spectacular and lengthy media coverage of this man who accepted concurrently the titles of "Satan," "devil" and "god."

18

A temporary "fad" of a small section of the youth subculture, you say? Society on the whole *is* rational and scientific, you say? How then does one account for the fact that Peter Hurkos, the clairvoyant who worked on the Boston Strangler case, was one of the first men called to investigate the Sharon Tate mansion after the infamous murders committed there? Called, I may add, by the "establishment"!

"A spiritual or mystical revival is taking place in society at large," proclaims Edward B. Fiske in analyzing the new trend for the *New York Times*. "It can be seen in increased interest in the occult, Eastern religion, and primitive practices such as witchcraft . . ."[14]

Life magazine's London staff writer, Arturo Gonzalez, Jr., adds in amazement that "despite the fact that more than two fifths of the American population goes to church every week, as do almost half of its college students, fascination with the black sciences is apparently at an all-time high.[15]

In a day when astrologers are paid as much as Wall Street bankers, when mediums are regularly consulted by government officials and when thousands of "Christians" leave their churches for covens, we do well to think seriously about the current occult explosion.

The German professor Adolf Koberle has, at best, understated the problem when he writes, "Our age is, in an eminent measure a distraught, insecure time."[16]

Footnotes for Chapter 2

1. Richard Cavendish, *Newsweek,* August 21, 1967, p. 66.

2. Arturo F. Gonzalez, Jr., "The Witchcraft Revival," *Christian Herald,* June 1970, p. 27.

3. Gonzalez, "The Witchcraft Revival," p. 25.

4. S.K. Oberbeck, "Double, Double," *Newsweek,* August 21, 1967, p. 66.

5. J. Rohler, "What's the Mutter With Astrology?" *Christianity Today,* November 21, 1969, p. 42.

6. Richard Cavendish, *Man, Myth and Magic,* 7 volumes. (Great Britain: Purnell, Inc., 1970), vol. 1, no. 1, p. 1.

7. "How Quackery Thrives on the Occult," *Today's Health,* November 1970, p. 22.

8. Tom Burke, "Princess Leda's Castle in the Air," *Esquire,* March 1970, pp. 104-107.

9. Burke, *Esquire,* p. 112.

10. Hanz Holzer, *The Truth About Witchcraft* (Garden City, N.Y.: Doubleday, 1969), p. 235.

11. *The Detroit Free Press,* May 25, 1967.

12. Judith Rascoe, "The Church of Satan," *McCall's,* March 1970, p. 133.

13. For further reading: Kurt Koch, D.D., *Between Christ and Satan* (Berghausan BD. Germany, Evangelization Publishers, 1961), p. 79ff. U.S. edition: Grand Rapids: Kregel Publications, 1968.

14. E.P. News Service, April 18, 1970, La Canada, California.

15. Gonzalez, "The Witchcraft Revival."

16. Adolf Koberle, "Glaube Oder Aberglaube," *Schrift and Bekenntnis,* 1961, p. 106.

19

"*I swear there ain't no heaven, but pray there ain't no hell.*"

Blood, Sweat & Tears
And When I Die

CHAPTER 3

Rosemary's Grandchildren

Suppose a friend came up to you and said, "Hey, you won't believe this, but . . ." and then proceeded to relate an experience of the night before when he had been invited to observe a real witchcraft coven —complete with high priests, nude participants and ceremonial rituals.

Unlikely and a bit pretentious, you say?

Maybe so. But how would you respond when your friend countered your disbelief with, "If you don't believe me, why not come with me next week and see for yourself?"

Why does an invitation to a seance or a witchcraft meeting have such appeal? Such is certainly not the case with a similar invitation to a political rally or P.T.A. meeting, much less a church service.

I can't begin to count the number of young people and students with whom I have spoken, who have at some time or another used a Ouija board in jest and wound up shocked at the amazingly accurate answers to their questions. In the same way, the latest statistics show that more than 40 million Americans dare not leave their homes without first consulting their horoscope.[1]

Curiosity, amusement, fear, searching for truth, social pressure—who knows why a person first becomes interested in the occult. Suffice it to say that for whatever reason, people are opening themselves up more than ever before to the possibility of reality in the unseen world.

The mood of Britain and America over the past few years has been one of fearful uncertainty concerning the supernatural. The "spirit of the times" was ripe for occultism in the late sixties. Early Beatle records were being played backward and at different speeds, while the album covers were scrutinized for black walrus, bare feet and black carnations (all thought to be "death symbols" of the supposedly "late" Paul McCartney).

To what can we attribute the sudden increase of interest in the occult?

Many have speculated on this question, and their myriad answers are as diverse as the various forms of occultism. Generally speaking the one thing that most mystics and parapsychologists agree upon is the basic need for a "spiritual orientation" within each individual.

24

There are still among us, however, those who would disagree that there is an unseen world of spiritual forces in the universe. They believe only in what they can see with their eyes or touch with their body. As one advocate of this school of thought has said, man should act as though demons and unseeable forces do not exist—"until such a time as their existence is forced upon us!"[2]

That time is right here, right now!

Baudelaire once observed that "the Devil's cleverest wile is to convince us that he does not exist."[3] And often the best way to conceal the real significance and dynamic of a philosophy is to make a "fad" out of it. After all, we have been taught that the only thing permanent is change, and what is "in" today will be obsolete tomorrow! So magic, witchcraft and fortune-telling have become popularized, much to the dismay of their true followers.

To stay or not to stay?

As occultism has grown as a fad around the world, opinions have generally polarized into two separate camps. The skeptics have branded all occult phenomena as a "passing fancy" and tend to disregard any possibility of there being evil spirits such as the Bible says exist. "This too will pass" is their slogan, and they bury their heads in the sands of ignorance and disbelief.

The second camp consists of thousands of people around the world who have been sucked into occultism because of their delving into "fads" such as witchcraft and fortune-telling. There are countless stories of young people whose lives have been completely perverted because of an interest and experimentation in the occult. It all begins, perhaps, with the frequent use of a Ouija board or a Tarot deck. Innocent enough pastimes to while away the boring evening hours. All too often the end is a mental breakdown or actual demon possession.

Countless thousands are reaching out for more than their empirical reasoning can give them. "I'm looking for someone to change my life," echoes one of today's pop tunes. "I'm looking for a miracle in my life."[4]

As Ed Ames once sang,

"From the canyons of the mind we wander on and stumble blindly
Through the often tangled maze of starless nights and sunless days,
While asking for some kind of clue, a road to lead us to the truth,
But who will answer?
Is our hope in walnut shells worn 'round the neck with temple bells,
Or deep within some cloistered walls where hooded figures pray in halls,
Or from old books on dusty shelves, or in the stars, or in ourselves?
Who will answer?"[5]

In the midst of a sterile and scientific world, a stainless-steel culture, a man cries out for the reality behind the mask. Searching in the midst of imitations for the real, the authentic.

It is the "desacrilizing" of a society, as Bishop Lesslie Newbegin has stated,[6] that will turn it into a happy hunting ground for astrologers, necromancers, cultists and black magicians, for a man is incurably religious and he knows that to become secular (i.e., nonreligious) is really to die.

"In the heart of every man," said the French scientist and philosopher Blaise Pascal, "there is a God-shaped vacuum which only God can fill through His Son, Jesus Christ."

In a generation of philosophical existentialism, we often find it unnatural, if not impossible, to believe that the God of our fathers has survived the generations. That this same God is eternal and unchangeable. That this same God created man in His image, not the reverse. It is easier to mistake pragmatism for reality—to believe only in that which we can see, feel, taste, touch and smell.

It is the conviction of this author that God is alive and well. Beyond that, that He is knowable not through logical reasoning nor through scientific investigation nor through mystic revelation, but through faith as outlined in the New Testament. It is this personal faith that goes beyond the ritual, that answers the basic questions of man.

"What we are witnessing today is irrationality among people who can't stand up to the pressures of incessant change," says Jan Ehrenwald, consulting psychiatrist at Roosevelt Hospital in New York. "It's an expression of the chaotic state of our civilization, the loss of spiritual and religious values.'

In speaking of the increased interest in the unknown, Hanz Holzer, author of *The Truth About Witchcraft*, states that "religion in the traditional sense no longer provides the spiritual guidance and

27

sustenance in times of trouble it used to. . . . People get divorced and people pray and get no answers and people are hurt by other people and the churches just stand by and say, 'Well, there's nothing you can do, really, old boy, it's part of God's will.' "[8] He continues by saying that even though these things might be God's will, people leave their church and go in search of "something else to fill their spiritual void. For man cannot long endure without some sort of spiritual crutch or faith."[9]

So right he is! Organized religion—man's attempt to reach God—is no longer the crutch it used to be. The important difference is that crutches are man-made, while saving faith is God-given! True faith begins with belief in the fact that God reached down in human history to make contact with man.

Merely because a thing is a product of a power beyond the mind's invention does not necessarily mean it is "of God."

The two worlds

Though this book is not intended to be an apologetic for the reality of the occult, we shall let the evidence speak for itself. The Bible clearly speaks of two separate personalities in the realm of the supernatural, God the superior, and Satan the inferior. To view the powers behind the universe, nature and conscience in any other frame of reference is a strain on the imagination, as well as an unjustifiable rationalization.

Thomas Howard summarizes the Christian's position as follows: "Any Christian is committed to the notion of a universe, first of all, that is put together according to a Supreme Design, and in which nothing is mere random; and second, to one that is full of actual, personified war between good and evil. The story of St. Michael the Archangel and Satan is not just a vivid way of picturing the struggle between abstract forces; it touches on the truth of the matter far more accurately than astronomy or psychology."[10]

The non-Christian must agree that the search for God takes on many forms—the present interest in the occult being one of these. As St. Augustine observed, "Thou hast made us for Thyself, O God, and our hearts are restless until they find their rest in Thee."

Each person must make a choice concerning the realm of the supernatural. The Bible says that we either serve God—or we serve Satan. There is no middle ground—no neutral territory.

In his excellent book, *The Screwtape Letters,* C.S. Lewis reminds us, "There are two equal and opposite errors into which our race can fall about the devils. One is to disbelieve in their existence. The other is to believe, and to feel an excessive and unhealthy interest in them." He continues to add, "They themselves are equally pleased by both errors and hail a materialist or a magician with the same delight."[11]

Hopefully, the subsequent chapters will stay within these boundaries.

Footnotes for Chapter 3

1. Isabella Taves, "Astrology, Fun, Fraud, or Keyhole to the Future?" *Look* magazine, May 13, 1969, p. 98.

2. Henry Ansgar Kelly, in his recent book, *The Devil, Demonology and Witchcraft,* attempts to thoroughly discredit the traditional church's position on the reality of a personal Satan and his devils. Kelly holds that the biblical record is riddled with myths, legends and cultural tradition which have since been explained by modern medicine and psychiatry. He leaves himself an "out," though, by suggesting that man should act as though demons do not exist, *"until such a time as their existence is forced upon us"!*

3. "The Priest's Rebellion," *Newsweek* magazine, November 11, 1968, p. 71.

4. Moody Blues, "Question," Threshold Records.

5. Ed Ames, "Who Will Answer?" *(Aleluya No. 1)* R.C.A. Victor.

6. J. Rohler, "What's the Mutter with Astrology?" *Christianity Today,* November 21, 1969, p 43.

7. "How Quackery Thrives on the Occult," *Today's Health,* November 1970, p. 87.

8. Hanz Holzer, *The Truth About Witchcraft* (Garden City, N.Y.: Doubleday, 1969), p. 32.

9. Holzer, *The Truth About Witchcraft,* p. 33.

10. Thomas Howard, "Those Witches Keep Cropping Up," *Apocalypse,* August 24, 1970, pp. 2, 3.

11. C. S. Lewis, *The Screwtape Letters* (New York: The Macmillan Co., 1943), preface p. 13.

PART TWO
MANTIC

"*Forget your hexagram, you'll soon feel fine.*
Stop lookin' at the stars, you don't live under the signs.
Don't mess with gypsies, or have your fortune read,
Keep your table on the floor, and don't you listen to the dead."

Larry David Norman
Upon This Rock

CHAPTER 4

Horror-Scopes

Did you feel any better this morning when you woke up than you did yesterday? Is life treating you better this year than last?

It should. According to astrologers, that is.

You see, this is the dawning of the "Age of Aquarius," and to most stargazers, a time when "the moon is in the seventh house, and Jupiter aligns with Mars." So "peace will guide the planets, and love will steer the stars." According to the rock musical "Hair," this is the way things should be because the stars have decreed it.

Those "in the know" concerning astrology are not in agreement, however, as to whether or not the Age of Aquarius has really begun in earnest. Some say it began with the French Revolution, others think it started in the early 1900s, while still others are predicting it for the year 2000. But the general idea is that we are leaving the "Age of Pisces," characterized by tears and sorrow, and entering the age of "golden living dreams of visions, and the mind's true liberations."[1]

Astrology is the religion of the day. Dr. Kurt Koch, in fact, has called astrology "the most widely spread superstition of our time."[2] Over 40 million Americans trust in the stars. Ten thousand full-time and 175,000 part-time professional astrologers in the U.S. have turned the zodiac into a $200 million-a-year business.[3]

Astrology is so widespread that we often can't see the forest for the trees. Many people already accept horoscopes and astrological readings as a way of life. When the Beatles formed their recording company, "Apple," they hired a full-time astrologer to chart the course of their endeavors. The rock musical "Hair" had its own staff astrologer and businessmen throughout the country enlist the services of professional astrologers.

An IBM computer shoots out over 30,000 "personalized" horoscopes every month to shoppers in department stores from coast to coast. Costing each subscriber from $20 to $50 per year, the computer digests 25 million pieces of information and then gives each client 15 to 20 pages of analytical and prophetic utterances. If one particular computerized horoscope disagrees with or offends the client, there is still hope, for three such computer firms are currently competing for the business.

There is also a 24-hour-a-day Zodiatronics telephone service and another company which places computer horoscopes on 2,000 college campuses nationwide. Astroflash, Inc. processes about 500 horoscopes a day in New York's Grand Central Station and is planning to open several other branches, since business is doing so well.[4]

Any market or bookstore you walk into is bound to offer you such pertinent works as *Astrology for Everyday Living, Astrology Made Practical, Astrology Answers Your Questions, Your Character in the Stars and Astrology and Your Destiny.*

You can also pursue special interest fields with *Your Baby's First Horoscope, Astrology for Teens* and *How to Find Your Mate Through Astrology.* If that's not enough, you can cook, diet, raise dogs, cats and racehorses all by using the appropriate astrological guide.

It looks like the era of the do-it-yourself personality of Dale Carnegie has given way to the let-the-stars-do-it-for-you philosophy of Carroll Righter. Carroll Righter is reputedly paid in four figures by some celebrities who retain him yearly for immediate astrological advice.[5]

The twelve signs of the zodiac have been made into necklaces, rings, earrings, belts, shoe ornaments, key chains, car emblems, plaques, trophies and even underwear!

While conservative business firms like Abraham and Straus retain full-time astrologers, *Life* magazine reports that a member of the New York Stock Exchange "likes to conclude important deals at 3 A.M. because of his astrologer's counsel."[6]

Faced with these astounding facts and figures, one question raises itself: Why? Why all the interest in the art and practice of astrology? Why are people turning to horoscope readings for security and advice? Is it all superstition? Or are these people really searching for that "something" which they feel astrology gives them?

"If you wait to buy a house until Mercury and Jupiter are in certain positions in the sky," explains Richard Cavendish, author of *The Black Arts*, "you are following a procedure which is just as magical as the medieval cure for lunacy which prescribes tying a herb round the patient's neck with a red cloth when the moon is waxing in the sign of Taurus. In one case the moon's influence is used to cure a lunatic, in the other the influences of Mercury and Jupiter are used to secure a satisfactory house. Most people who believe in astrology would probably reject the medieval lunacy cure, but if they are consistent they should not doubt it because it smacks of magic."[7]

Like many other "religions" which man clings to in his search for truth, astrology's history goes back to the early history of the human race.

The history of astrology

For thousands of years man has turned to the stars and the heavens as a source of inspiration and guidance. In the book of Genesis, we encounter an astrology buff who lived over four thousand years ago.[8] Nimrod, the first "world dictator," had in mind a universal language and shrine dedicated to the national pursuit of astrology. (At that time, incidentally, there was no difference between astronomy and astrology. In fact, astrology was considered one of the most important sciences in Babylonian culture. Every ruler had his own staff of astrologers; the more, the better, since the number of astrologers was a political status symbol.)

Nimrod decided to build his tower on a plain in the land of Shinar. The tower was constructed so that its "top *will reach* into heaven" (v. 4). The words "will reach" are in italics because they are not part of the original Hebrew text. Literally translated, the passage reads "whose top represents the heavens." In other words, the builders realized that they could not build a skyscraper which would actually scrape the sky. If they had that in mind, they would have moved the construction site a few miles to the top of one of the nearby hills, thus giving them a head start of several hundred feet into the sky. What they were building was a tower of astrological worship.

The ruins of this Babylonian tower are still in existence today. It still rises to a height of 153 feet above the plain from a base covering a square of 400 feet, or almost four acres, according to Dr. E. A. Wallis Budge of the British Museum. It was constructed of kiln-dried bricks in seven stages to correspond with the planets to which they were dedicated: the lowermost, black, the color of Saturn; the next, orange for Jupiter and the third, red for Mars.

These stages were surmounted by a lofty tower on the summit of which, we are told, were the signs of the zodiac and other astronomical figures.

In astrology's first days thousands of years ago, it was a science for the priests only. Horoscopes were cast for kings alone. Ruins in Mexico have disclosed that at the same time that astrology was booming in Babylon, people in the western hemisphere were studying the influence of the stars and planets. For this reason, many scientists and psychologists believe that astrology, the search of the stars for an answer to life's riddles, is a phenomenon that is common to all men in all cultures.

The zodiac is perhaps one of the oldest philosophic concepts of mankind. It is generally agreed upon by researchers that the great pyramids in Egypt were built in line with astrological calculations. By constructing the main passageway leading down to the king's chamber on an angle, the early architects allowed the rays of the polar star of that age to shine down the passage and rest upon the sarcophagus in the center of the chamber.[9]

After enjoying great popularity in the Chaldea area for several hundred years, astrology was finally dismissed by many as being more trickery than anything else. Moving from the Medo-Persian Empire, it traveled to Greece, where Alexander the Great was trying to amalgamate the East and the West into one kingdom under his authority. It was here, in Greece, that Ptolemy fully developed it into a "science." It was also here that Greek and Roman mythology were made an integral part of the astrological faith. Of course, even in Roman days there were a number of skeptics as to its ability to chart the course of human events. The Roman poet Ennius is quoted as saying, "Horoscopes cost one drachme, and are one drachme too expensive."[10]

Most of the Caesars, history also records, had their own personal "augurs" or astrologers. Had Julius taken the advice of one of his augurs, who knows what might have happened! He might have stayed home on the "Ides of March" and changed the fate of Rome.

In ancient China, astrology was in vogue until 2154 B.C., when astrologers Hi and Ho were deposed for their failure to predict a solar eclipse. In the East, the Hindu writers on astrology included men like Garga, Parashara and Mihina.

Writer Joseph Bayley suggests that an astronomer-priest may have been responsible for the mysterious Stonehenge ruins that have stood silent for 800 years on Salisbury Plain in southern England. The same type of priest probably constructed the elaborate pre-Columbian Nazca sand drawings, with their calendar of the skies, clearly visible from the air.[11]

The so-called "astrological science" continued from its Babylonian beginnings to the Reformation. During the Middle Ages, Europe was in the grip of astrological influence. Emperors subscribed to it and professorial chairs in the universities were created for astrological scholars. Geoffrey Chaucer was considered to be an excellent astrologer. His poem "Canterbury Tales" abounds in astrological symbolism. (One noted astrologer of the day predicted that a flood would sweep over the continent

41

in February of 1524. The population was terrified, and no one would work. Many tried to escape with ships or fled into the nearby mountains. But the flood never came. The stars—and the stargazer—were wrong!)

It was not until the "Age of Reason," about 1750, that there was a definite split between astrology and astronomy. St. Augustine, a former devotee of astrology, was one of many who became disenchanted with it and turned to biblical Christianity. Augustine thereafter referred to astrology as "the craziest delusion of mankind."[12] Rapidly losing its following as well as its integrity, astrology remained a little-practiced art until its revival in Britain and France about 1890 and in Germany about 1930.

Astrology today is approaching a new height of popularity. In India the religion of astrology still has a tight grasp upon the populace. Many of the other nations of the world that are immersed in Hinduism are also steeped in astrology. Marriages may not take place unless the stars are in alignment —business ventures wait to be completed until the planets give the go-ahead.

Astrologers have connected almost every important event of mankind with the stars. Both the birth and death of Julius Caesar were accompanied by comets; and Wellington's defeat of Napoleon at Waterloo has been astrologically traced to the positions of Jupiter at Wellington's birth and Saturn at Napoleon's. World War I was ushered in with solar and lunar eclipses and the American involvement in World War II was triggered, it is said, by the movements of Mars and Uranus.

42

How astrology works

In our search for the "why" of astrology's long-lasting popularity, we must examine the basic tenets of this religion. What does astrology teach about man and his relationship to the universe around him? Why is it that so many people have fallen under the spell of the stars?

In the Mesopotamiam Valley of five or six thousand years ago, astrology was viewed differently than it is today. It was concerned at that time mainly with events affecting whole nations and peoples, not primarily with the personal lives of individuals. It was not until the Greeks that the mythological elements were added and astrologers became concerned with the fate of individual men and women. The earlier form of astrology, national in scope, is called *mundane*, while the popular version today, dealing with the charting of individual lives, is called *natal* astrology.

Shakespeare's "star-crossed lovers," Romeo and Juliet, are prime examples of *natal* astrology. Each born under a different sign, it was believed their fates were already cast at the time of their births.

Upon closer investigation, one discovers that the "zodiac," or imaginary belt of the heavens, is divided into houses, each containing a different constellation. There are twelve divisions, each one being equal. Each house or "sign" is ruled by a planet, the sun also having been considered by the Babylonians to be a planet. One born under a particular sign, it is believed, inherits the general personality of that sign. *Capricorn* (December 22-January 19) is the Goat; *Aquarius* (January 20-February 18) is the Water-bearer; *Pisces* (February 19-March 20) is the Fish; *Aries* (March 21-April 19) is the Ram; *Taurus* (April 20-May 20) is the Bull; *Gemini* (May 21-June 21) is the Twins; *Cancer*[13] (June 22-July 22) is the Crab; *Leo* (July 23-August 22) is the Lion; *Virgo* (August 23-September 22) is the Virgin; *Libra* (September 23-October 23) is the Scales; *Scorpio* (October 24-November 21) is the Scorpion; and *Sagittarius* (November 22-December 21) is the Archer. Thus, it is said that Aquarians have a totally different personality than do Virgos, and each is recognizable according to the traits within each sign.

A horoscope (Greek, "hour-watcher") is the chart of the positions of the planets in relationship to one another at the exact time of your birth. Astrologers maintain that your personality and your future both can be determined by where each planet in the heavens was the second you were brought into this world. Your fate, then, was sealed the moment you were born and nothing can change it. Of course, astrologers do say that you can avoid bad days and take advantage of good ones if you know ahead of time when they are coming. And this, as one might expect, is what you pay an astrologer to do for you! With promised accuracy, he can "chart" the course of your life for you so that you always know what to expect and when to expect it.

Fate—the name of the game

Somewhere in the recesses of each man's mind is

the desire to know what life is all about. It is easy to see why astrology appeals to so many people. Not willing to trust an all-powerful, all-knowing Creator, they turn instead to the seemingly easy way out. "It's in the stars," many people cry out with assurance. A desire to know the future, a desire to make the universe work for man, a desire to rely upon something stable and trustworthy, a desire to play God—all these factors go into making astrology the popular religion that it is.

The person who refuses to acknowledge the existence and authority of a divine being might seriously consider pursuing astrology—after all, he needs all the help he can get. But there is a better way—that of a loving, personal God who alone has control over all the future and holds mankind in the palm of His hand.

The Bible unequivocally condemns astrology as evil. As early as the writing of the book of Deuteronomy God pronounced His judgment on astrologers and those who seek answers in the heavens: "If there is found in your midst, in any of your towns, which the Lord your God is giving you, a man or a woman who does what is evil in the sight of the Lord your God, by transgressing His covenant, and has gone and served other gods and worshiped them, or the sun or the moon or any of the heavenly host, which I have not commanded; and if it is told you and you have heard of it, then you shall inquire thoroughly. And behold, if it is true and the thing certain that this detestable thing has been done in Israel, then you shall bring out that man or that woman who has done this evil deed, to your gates, that is, the man or the woman, and you shall stone them to death."[14] There was no light penalty assessed to those who worshiped the heavens rather than the Creator—the sentence was death by stoning.

Since the early astrologers encouraged people to worship the planets rather than the Creator of the planets, astrology was a form of idol worship, and thereby a transgression of the first commandment of God, "You shall have no other gods before Me."[15]

A Christian should avoid astrology because it places God's creation ahead of God.

The Bible declares that God created the planets and the stars and that He is the One responsible for the course of events, not the heavenly bodies themselves. We are to consider the Creator rather than His creation. "When I consider Thy heavens, the work of Thy fingers, the moon and the stars, which Thou has ordained."[16] In looking to these, man has taken his eyes off of the power and the glory behind them.

Astrologers and stargazers are fallible and often inaccurate, whereas God is perfect in His revelations of the secrets of the universe. "As for the mystery about which the king has inquired, neither wise men, conjurers, magicians, nor diviners are able to declare it to the king. However, there is a God in heaven who reveals mysteries, and He has made known to King Nebuchadnezzar what will take place in the latter days."[17]

As a science, astrology is unscientific. When the zodiac was charted in ancient days, it was based upon the concept that the stars, sun and planets revolved around the earth. The Copernican theory of the heavens has disproved this theory, but many astrologers work with zodiac charts which are still based upon these antiquated concepts. Also, planets which have been discovered in recent years (Uranus in 1781, Neptune in 1839, and Pluto in 1932) seem to have little bearing on a person's horoscope, even though the charts were constructed before the discovery of these planetary bodies.[18]

Astrology is often a deceptive and fraudulent practice. One newspaper editor even admits that he used old horoscopes every so often in his daily zodiac column without anyone being the wiser. Many "forecasts" are created by people who are anxious to capitalize on the popularity of the movement and the gullibility of its adherents. For example, in reading my Pisces forecast from three different astrologers on any given day, I may be faced with either watching my spending habits, watching my wife or taking a long voyage! Astrology has been a million dollar market in recent years, and its deception is monumental.

Despite Carroll Righter's statement that "the stars impel; they do not compel,"[19] the follower of present-day astrology must, of necessity, put his faith in fate rather than in God. Astrology, because it is fatalistic in its approach to the future and the free will of mankind, is opposed to the biblical teaching that man chooses his own destiny (based largely upon his acceptance or rejection of the living God).

Dr. Kurt Koch, in his book *Between Christ and*

Satan, tells the case history of a woman who "appeared at a police station and stated that she had just killed her son by shooting him. An astrologer had told her in a horoscope that her son would never regain his full mental health. Wanting to save the boy from this terrible future, she had killed him. The woman was arrested and finally sentenced after a long trial. The astrologer himself went free."[20] Here we have a perfect example of the fatalism inherent in astrology. Because the woman firmly believed that nothing could change the fate of her son, she fell victim to playing God and took his future in her own hands.

Scientists and psychologists also maintain that there is a high degree of autosuggestion involved in astrology. If someone tells you that something is going to happen to you, the idea becomes planted in your subconscious mind. And sure enough, you make that event happen by setting yourself up for it! Once the suggestion is firmly rooted in the mind, its prediction often comes true because you allow it to do so.[21]

These, then, are the main reasons why the Christian especially should avoid pursuing astrology. Unfortunately, the tendency for most people is to take astrology too lightly. Comments like "It's not that bad," or "I don't really believe it; it's just for fun," reveal the spiritual ignorance of the consequences of dabbling in astrology. "For as he thinks within himself, so he is,"[22] the Bible says. Dr. Schrank, the medical superintendent of Wiesbaden, writes in an article about the psychology of superstition, "How dangerous the effects of astrology are

48

is proved by the fact that in sensitive people serious psychic disturbances, fear of life, despair and disorders have been observed. Astrology paralyzes initiative and power of judgment. It stupefies and encourages shallowness. It uniforms the personality for a platitudinous underground movement."[23]

Astrology might, on the surface, seem to make life a lot simpler—just relaxing in some "cosmic fatalism." Some might even foolishly believe that God would reveal His will for them through the stars.

Such thinking is mere rationalization. God created man in His image, with personal initiative and creativity, and free will. He has good reason for keeping the future to Himself. Jesus summed it up when He said, "Do not be anxious for tomorrow; for tomorrow will care for itself. Each day has enough trouble of its own."[24]

Told in the heavens

But while both *mundane* and *natal* astrology offer unacceptable alternatives, there is a third possibility. Contrary to popular opinion, it might very well be that God has, in the past, used the heavens to communicate with man.

The Bible states that "Because that which is known about God is evident within them; for God made it evident to them. For since the creation of the world His invisible attributes, His eternal power and divine nature have been clearly seen, being understood through what has been made so that they are without excuse."[25] The "invisible things" could be interpreted as God's plans and

49

purposes—at least they are evidences of His power as Creator God. One might rightly ask how could these things be known by men? How could man have known anything about the God of the Bible before the Bible was written?

Paul states that "So faith comes from hearing, and hearing by the Word (i.e., 'the thing spoken, the sayings') of Christ. . . . Surely they have never heard, have they? Indeed they have: 'Their voice has gone out into all the earth, and their words (i.e., "message, instruction") to the ends of the world.' "[26]

The answer is unavoidable; the "invisible things" of God can be known by the heavens. This is substantiated when we understand that the writer is quoting from Psalm 19.

Notice the words of this song of David:

"The heavens are telling of the glory of God; and
    the firmament is declaring the work of
    His hands.
Day to day pours forth speech,
"Lift up your eyes—And night to night reveals
    knowledge.
There is no speech, nor are there words;
Their voice is not heard.
Their line has gone out through all the earth,
And their utterances to the end of the world.
In them He has placed a tent for the sun,
Which is as a bridegroom coming out of his
    chamber;
It rejoices as a strong man to run his course.
Its rising is from one end of the heavens,
And its circuit to the other end of them;

And there is nothing hid from its heat."[27]

The psalm is filled with astrological terms and symbolism. The names of several stars and constellations are mentioned even as far back in history as the book of Job, thought to be the oldest book in the Bible.

The prophet Isaiah commanded,

"Lift up your eyes on high and see who has created these stars,

The one who leads forth their host by number

He calls *them all by name*

Because of the greatness of His might and the strength of His power

Not one of them is missing."[28]

David proclaimed, "He counts the number of the stars; He gives names to all of them."[29]

The great historian Flavius Josephus quotes eight ancient gentile authorities as stating that "God gave the antediluvians such long life that they might perfect those things which they had invented in astronomy."[30] Casini begins his *History of Astronomy* by stating, "It is impossible to doubt that astronomy was invented from the beginning of the world; history, profane as well as sacred, testifies to this truth."[31]

The God of the Bible is also the God of the Heavens. God's message and teachings are shown in the heavens.[32] It seems logical to assume that God placed the stars in position as He wished, and through this, revealed to man any message He desired. It is not being suggested, however, that God created the zodiac and, therefore, astrology in its present form.

Let me quickly say that the astrology of today is in no way the same as the "astrology" of creation. A heavenly revelation of God's plan in the stars was only necessary until He provided a written one. The Greeks followed those before them in perverting the true message of God by interpreting it in the light of their man-made mythology.

Many today believe that Christianity and the Bible have evolved from one or more of the ancient religions, including the oldest of all, astrology. In light of the testimony of Scripture itself, this could not possibly have been the case. Rather, astrology as we know it today had its roots in the "astrology" of God. Because man by nature rejected the idea of a personal God who created the universe for His glory, he began to worship the heavens rather than worship the God who created them. Man demanded more than signs. He wanted something visible to worship.

Exactly what the "signs" were is not known. It is thought by many, including this author, that the zodiac constellations foresaw the birth, death, resurrection, and Second Coming of Christ.

The brilliant Christian scholar E. W. Bullinger expands more fully on this idea in his work, *The Witness of the Stars*. As Mr. Bullinger clearly points out, the stars present systematically the plan of God for the redemption of sinful man. Beginning with the constellation Virgo, "the Virgin" (indicating the Promised Seed of the woman), and continuing through the twelve "houses" to Leo, "The Lion" (suggesting the eventual overthrow of the enemy by the Lion of the Tribe of Judah), the stars give witness to the person and work of Jesus Christ, the Son of God.

Considering the fact that mankind had existed for at least 2,500 years before any written revelation from God, it is probable that God revealed His plan of salvation through the heavenly constellations. Both Zacharias[33] and the apostle Peter[34] reaffirm this conviction in speaking of the "holy prophets" which have been "since the world began."

Almighty God beautifully set forth in star pictures the story of the supernatural events which would take place on this planet—those surrounding the birth, death and resurrection of Christ and those surrounding His second coming and final rule. There is no doubt but that God gave man the "figures" in astronomy as a revelation of His Word— from the Virgin with child[35] all the way through to the Lion with his foot resting upon the head of the serpent.[36]

God has revealed, in both the heavens and the holy Scriptures, His plan of salvation for mankind. His reason has always been "so that they were without excuse"[37] who reject His offer of eternal salvation.

The Bible promises that one day God will create a "new heaven and a new earth; for the first heaven and the first earth passed away."[38] Astrology, therefore, is not eternal. One day "the stars of heaven and their constellations will not flash forth their light; the sun will be dark when it rises, and the moon will not shed its light."[39] When that happens, what good will zodiacs and horoscopes do mankind? "Let now the astrologers, those who prophesy by stars, those who predict by the new moons, stand up and save you from what will come upon you."[40] The Bible says the astrologers will not even be able to save themselves, much less their many followers.

The One who *can* save man, direct his future and provide daily fulfillment is the One of whom the stars have been clearly speaking for centuries.

Footnotes for Chapter 4

1. "Age of Aquarius" by the 5th Dimension, Soul City Records.

2. Kurt Koch, D.D., *Between Christ and Satan* (Berghausan BD. Germany, Evangelization Publishers, 1961), p. 14. U.S. edition: Grand Rapids: Kregel Publications, 1968.

3. "How Quackery Thrives on the Occult," *Today's Health*, November 1970, p. 21. (Cf. "Mysticism and the Occult" by Lester L. Grabbe, *Plain Truth* magazine, vol. 36, no. 1. November 1971, p. 38.)

4. Judith Rascoe, "The Age of Occult," *McCall's* magazine, March 1970, p. 61.

5. Isabella Taves, "Astrology, Fun, Fraud, or Keyhole to the Future?" *Look* magazine, May 13, 1969, p. 98.

6. Joseph Bayley, *What About Horoscopes?* (Elgin, Ill.: David C. Cook, Publishers, 1970), p. 8.

7. Richard Cavendish, *The Black Arts* (New York: G. P. Putnam & Sons, 1967), p. 219.

8. Genesis 11.

9. Eden Gray, *A Complete Guide to the Tarot* (New York: Crown Publishers, 1970), p. 137.

10. Koch, *Between Christ and Satan*, pp. 14, 15.

11. Bayley, *What About Horoscopes?* p. 13.

12. Koch, *Between Christ and Satan*, p. 15.

13. Renamed by famed astrologer Carroll Righter "moon children."

14. Deuteronomy 17:2-5.

15. Exodus 20:3.

16. Psalm 8:3.

17. Daniel 2:27, 28.

18. See discussion of this error in Daniel Cohen's *Myths of the Space Age* (New York: Dodd, Mead & Co., 1967).

19. Cavendish, *The Black Arts*, p. 213.

20. Koch, *Between Christ and Satan*, pp. 13, 14.

21. Psychologist Carl Gustav Jung believed that a horoscope can shed light on certain "psychic imprints" with which a man is born. Jung frequently refers to the principle of "synchronicity" dealing with the "collective unconscious" mind. For further study, see "The Archetypes and the Collective Unconscious" *(Collected Works of Carl Gustav Jung;* vol. 9, pt. 1. New York: Pantheon Books, 1953-70).

22. Proverbs 23:7.

23. Koch, *Between Christ and Satan*, p. 22.

24. Matthew 6:34.

25. Romans 1:19,20.

26. Romans 10:17.

27. Psalm 19:1-6.

28. Isaiah 40:26.

29. Psalm 147:4.

30. Flavius Josephus in *The Witness of the Stars* by Ethelbert W. Bullinger, D.D. (Grand Rapids: Kregel Publications, 1967), p. 9. (Reproduced from the original edition published in London in 1893.)

31. Bullinger, *The Witness of the Stars*, p. 9.

32. Romans 1:19,20.

33. Zacharias in Luke 1:67-70, "As he spoke by the mouth of His holy prophets from of old."

34. Peter in Acts 3:20,21, "Which God spoke by the mouth of His holy prophets from ancient time."

35. Isaiah 7:14, a prophecy of the coming of Christ. (Cf. Matthew 1:23.)

36. In fulfillment of that day in the future when Christ shall "bruise you (Satan) on the head" (Genesis 3:15).

37. Romans 1:20.

38. Revelation 21:1.

39. Isaiah 13:10.

40. Isaiah 47:13.

"The soul goes round upon a wheel of stars and all things return ... Good and evil go round in a wheel that is one thing and not many. Do you not realize in your heart, do you not believe behind all your beliefs, that there is but one reality and we are its shadows; and that all things are but aspects of one thing; a centre where men melt into Man and Man into God?"

" 'No,' said Father Brown."

G. K. Chesterton
The Dagger with Wings

CHAPTER 5

Spook for Yourself

"Mirror, mirror, on the wall—who's the fairest of them all?"

A flash of lightning, a roar of thunder, a short earthquake and then came the answer. A spirit figure appeared in the mirror and revealed that it was Snow White who held the cherished beauty title. A bit angry, to say the least, the Wicked Witch took off toward Miss White's house with the poisoned apple designed to do her in.

The children's story went something like that, as I recall. As absurd as it might seem, the whole idea of mirrors talking was nothing new to the storyteller. Nor does that same mentality seem too absurd to thousands of intelligent people today.

Talking mirrors are only a few of the tools of the trade for those involved in the pursuit of mantic or "fortune-telling." Cards, tea leaves, pendulums, divining rods, crystal balls and Ouija boards are all considered indispensable "bridges" between the fortune-teller and the unknown future.

Like astrology, the art of "mantic" continues to flourish today.

Soothsayers are not only saying their sooth more now; they're flooding the market with it! Tarot cards, for example, can be purchased at almost any department or toy store in the country. One large department store chain in Los Angeles recently advertised a Tarot deck in their Christmas catalog as an "enlightening imaginative family game"! The cost for the deck? A mere six dollars. At almost any fair or outdoor bazaar, a tea-leaves reader or fortune-teller presents himself for those who pass by. For fifty cents or one dollar you can know if you will get a raise, marry your boyfriend or inherit a large sum of money.

Tarot cards

I guess my interest in fortune-telling first came into the open several years ago as a result of my fascination with the movie "The Magus." The film story was a compilation of bizarre magical rites, ghost appearances and a maze of mental gymnastics which prompted me to return to see it three different times. The title was taken from the Tarot card of the same name which means "magician."

So began nearly a year's involvement with one of the oldest fortune-telling devices of mankind, the Tarot cards. An adventure which I was later to regret.

It would perhaps be helpful, before continuing, to offer the following brief background and explanation of the Tarot cards.

Many occultists believe that the Tarot was invented by the ancient Egyptians as a repository for their occult lore and that they were introduced to Europe by the gypsies.[1] Differing traditions set the date of origin from sometime within the first century in ancient Rome to even as late as A.D. 1200 in Fez, Egypt. We probably can assume that they were widely used by pagan nations during the lifetime of Jesus Christ due to the strong Gnostic influence of that day, with its continual search for "spiritual" knowledge.

What probably began as a box of small clay tablets with obscure symbols is now available as a pack of 78 standard size picture cards still adorned with mysterious patterns and symbols. Divided into suits of Swords, Cups, Coins (or Pentacles) and Wands (or Staffs), it has been suggested by some that these suits are connected with the four sacred objects of the traditional Holy Grail legends—the sword, the cup, the dish and the lance. In addition to these "minor" cards, there are 22 others, called the "major trumps," each with a title below the figures.[2]

Like most people, I was unusually fascinated by the strangely grotesque illustrations on each of the cards. Examining the different medieval figures and landscapes is like remembering part of a dream. The main idea is unmistakable, though the particulars are not too clearly defined. There is the Fool with cap and bells, the Tower struck by lightning with the fiery Emperor and Empress falling toward the jagged cliffs below, the Hanged Man suspended upside down from a cross and the Devil pictured as a horned beast perched above and between a naked man and woman both of whom are horned and chained.

The true meaning of the Tarot deck is most uncertain. There are almost as many interpretations of the Tarot—occult, Christian, gypsy, psychological—as there are interpreters. Most occultists would probably agree with one modern researcher that "it may be that the deepest occult wisdom of the Tarot cannot be put into words after all" and "in the end, the seeker is told only what he cannot find for himself."[3]

The "power" of the Tarot cards, like any of the other objects of mantic, is to be found not in the object itself but in the power one gives it. This postulate holds true in all forms of fortune-telling. Whatever you put your faith in, will, to some extent and probability, work for you. The cards have no power but what the user gives to them by trusting in them. The issue is faith, not magic.

I was ignorant of the cards at the time I began to study and read them. It was a tedious project and rather awkward, with a Tarot deck in one hand and an instruction book in the other. After several preliminary tries, I jokingly asked the cards to "reveal" my future. To my complete astonishment, the reading was very close to what I knew to be true about my own character and personality.

More studying, more readings and finally I felt I was touching on something concrete, something that really worked. Each time I used the cards, I was a little more sure of myself.

Of course, I couldn't explain how they worked, but I figured it wasn't how they worked that was so important—it was what they said that was so intriguing.

I used the Tarot several times with friends and invariably found the readings to be more true than luck alone would allow. It was not until months after my original interest in the cards that I became suspect of the virtue of my endeavors.

I had finished reading an unusually depressing and alarming future for a friend when she asked to have another reading. Reluctantly I complied, assuring her that she couldn't believe *everything* in the cards. That it was, after all, more entertainment than reality. So I thought—until the second reading came out even clearer than the first and spoke of the same foretold events.

It was then that the woman informed me that she had received the same predictions from an accomplished card layer as well as from a palmist not long before our Tarot session. As expected, each of the predictions came about within a year of that incident.

To this day, I have not used the cards for a reading. Nor will I.

Fortune-telling with cards seems to have an unusual and unnatural appeal to the average person, especially among young people. I remember an incident that occurred after a session I had conducted with about 100 high schoolers on the subject of the occult. One of the students, a young man of about seventeen years of age, insisted on my letting him hold the Tarot deck. I hesitantly agreed and could not help noticing his total fascination with the cards. He interrupted me several times to ask how he would go about using them. Of course, I discouraged him from doing so and remarked that he must not have been listening to the lecture I had just given if he was still interested in any attempt to predict the future. I finally had to pry the cards from his hands when he stared glassy-eyed at me and calmly said, "I don't know what it is, but I have a strange feeling that I should sleep with these tonight."

The desire to know the future through the use of cards (cartomancy) is an increasingly strange phenomenon. Stores are often sold out of Tarot and Gypsy Witch decks and library shelves are perpetually empty of books on the subject. Of more concern is the fact that a great many Christians who claim to have a deep faith in a living God very often find themselves paying a card reader for advice. The following case study from Dr. Kurt Koch is typical of what can happen with cartomancy:

"A young Christian man told me about his time in the service. He was a corporal in a unit where the staff sergeant laid cards for all NCO's. At first the corporal objected to this fortune-telling. Finally he gave in to his superior. The card layer prophesied to him that the next day he would receive news of a death. He also could expect a money order during the next few days. As a matter of fact, the following day he received news that his uncle had died. Five days later he also received the announced money. The parents were never in the habit of sending their son money. It was a singular happening. After this session with the card layer, the corporal experienced depressions (melancholy thoughts). His prayer life was disturbed. He consulted a Christian man for counseling help. After the man prayed and laid hands on him the serious emotional disturbance disappeared completely."[4]

It is more than likely that the explanation of this incident lies not so much in the area of prevision or prophecy but in that of extrasensory perception (ESP). It is very possible that the corporal knew of his uncle's illness and feared his death. It is also possible that he assumed his parents would send him a note of congratulations and a monetary gift for his recent military honors. The card layer might very well have had an ability in ESP and been able to receive by telepathy the thoughts of the corporal.

A second question, however, deals with the mental and spiritual oppression the young man experienced after such an occurrence. Many, including myself, have had similar reactions to card readings (although the cure was not the same as in this illustration). It is here where one must decide to either limit himself to the normal or even paranormal explanations or else open his mind to the possibility of outer human, demonic powers oppressing or even obsessing the individual at such a time.

Palmistry

Palmistry is another form of mantic or fortune-telling. "Chiromancy" or palmistry—the art of discerning the future from the study of one's palm—can be traced back at least as far as ancient Rome and probably has roots much further back in human history. According to this occult belief, there are four main lines (heart, head, fate and life) as well as seven planet mounds (Mercury, Apollo, Saturn, Jupiter, Venus, Mars and Moon) on each person's palm.

The principle of fortune-telling through palmistry is the same as it is for card reading; only the objects are different. The palmist is much more limited in his impressions than the card layer, but the same forces are at work in both. In talking with scores of people who have consulted palmists, I seem to trace a definite pattern. Most of the experiences can be placed in one of three categories (or a combination of same). Either the palmist is a fraud and in it only for the quick money (which is often the case) or the palmist is sincere and genuinely gifted with an extrasensory ability or he has had a background in other areas of the occult and could easily be influenced by a spiritual demonic force.

There is a distinction between *chiromancy* (palmistry), *chirology* (the study of hand shape) and *graphology* (the interpretation of handwritin). Both chirology and graphology have some scientific substantiation; palmistry has none. Admittedly there is much fakery even in handwriting analysis, but that does not disprove what truth there is in the system. (I remember talking with a man once who built one of the first "computer handwriting analysis" machines. This particular model, along with several others patterned after it, was an impressive maze of dials, knobs, flashing lights and realistic computer cards but it was actually a gigantic "put-on." There were a half-dozen printed readings that would alternately fall into the final tray. So it really made no difference whose handwriting was being analyzed, the reading would be the same for every sixth customer.)

Numerology

Another type of fortune-telling is numerology. This study concerns itself with the numeric values of names and birthdates. Pythagoras, father of the present-day system of numerology, has been quoted as saying, "The world is built upon the power of numbers."[5]

The beginnings of the art go back deep into ancient history where a person's name was thought to be given by the gods and descriptive of his character. One's name, it was thought, is a tiny miniature of the person himself. In magical theory, it is believed that damaging or destroying another person's name transfers that same destruction onto the victim much like the practice used with Voodoo dolls. Egyptian tombs and Grecian temples have been found to contain pieces of lead, wax or pottery inscribed with names and curses. Apparently burying the name was a common way of wishing a death curse on the other person. Pounding a nail through the name was believed to bring about the same effect.

The hieroglyphs in Egyptian tombs express the same or similar ideas that the name *is* the person or thing. Animal hieroglyphs were often carved or painted in two separate halves for fear that if an exact representation were made, the beast would eat the food provided for the dead man or eat the dead man himself.

The importance of names is seen throughout the Old and New Testaments. Men, women and towns were given names descriptive of their function. For example, "Bethel" is "house of bread" and "Peter" means "rock." The Hebrew name for Jehovah, "Yahweh," was forbidden to be pronounced or even written down for fear that that which is holy would become profane.[6]

Still today a great importance is placed upon choosing just the right name for an infant. Numerous books and magazines are filled with listings of every conceivable name often with its root derivation and meaning. "Why were your parents so anxious to select a suitable name for you at the time of your birth?" asks a modern numerologist. "Because your name signifies your destiny and is the medium through which your character is expressed. It is the sign board or blueprint along your road to success. *Your parents sensed this and unconsciously named you for the particular character you were destined by birth to express.*"[7]

In a part of Jewish traditions, still practiced by some today, a child must never be named for a relative who is alive because it is believed that the relative will die if his name is taken for the child. In many fraternal and occult groups the initiate is given a "new" name—to be kept secret and used only within that particular fraternity. This is true of many of the Eastern religions as well. (About three years ago, my brother-in-law paid $35 to an Eastern mystic in return for which he received his own personal "word." A rather questionable practice at best, considering not one of the thousands of people who have received their "word" is able to tell it to anyone else!)

According to numerologists, a man's destiny is revealed to him through his name.[8] Each letter of the alphabet has its numeric equivalent from one to nine. By adding up each number in a commonly used name and reducing it to its one-digit equivalent, one is supposed to be able to determine his character, personality and destiny. For instance, the pseudonym MARILYN MONROE works out as follows: The total of the whole name (showing overall character) is two—the number of femininity. The vowel total (representing inner self) is three—brilliance, artistic ability, sparkle, charm, luck. The consonant total (outer personality) is eight—power, wealth, worldly involvement. Taking the most frequent letters in order, we get versatility, nervousness and restlessness as well as drive, ambition and ruthlessness. Loneliness and introspection follow, ending in unhappiness, defeat and the number two—the most ominous and evil of all numbers. Missing is the number six, which represents peace.

Applying these same rules of interpretation to my

own name, I come up with a basic number of six, meaning I am happy, equitable, kind, reliable and well-balanced. I don't really know what to do with my inner self, though, as it appears to be practical, uninspired and uninspiring while my outer self is said to be basically feminine! Needless to say, there are several contradictions within any given interpretation!

One of the obstacles to numerology is the fact that many people change their names later in life. This presents no problem to the sincere numerologist, however, because even the change is significant. For example, Napoleon Buonaparte changed his name later in life and numerologists believe, concurrently changed his destiny. In dropping the "u" from Buonaparte, he altered his number from one, standing for power and victory, to four, the number of defeat.

How much validity is there to numerology? Might I suggest that there is some truth in the idea that some numbers are symbolic in the Scriptures. The number one, for example, is often considered to be the number of wholeness and unity (i.e., one God, one church, one baptism). Three is thought to be completeness (the Trinity), while seven is perfection (as in the seven days of creation). The recurrence of certain numbers in Scripture, though, is of Holy design and in no way substantiates the present system of numerology.[9]

It is a wide stretch of the imagination that will accept the idea that when parents give their children names, they also plot destinies. The numerologists' rationale for this belief is linked to the same concept of cosmic life forces as are many other occult theories of mantic.

Divining rod and pendulum

The rod and the pendulum are further examples of man's quest for knowledge and power, especially knowledge of the future. Sticks, staffs and pendulums were used as mantic devices as early as the reign of the Chinese emperor Yu of the H-Sia Dynasty (2205 B.C.). Israel was warned against the pagan Canaanite practice of "rhabdomantic" or rod magic and tradition tells us that the Greeks, Romans, Scythians and Germanic peoples each had their rod conjurers. In the Middle Ages the rod and pendulum were used to locate ore veins and underground water sources. The modern users of the rod and pendulum attribute their success to what they term the principle of "radiaethesis" (i.e. the science of radiation). Societies and labor unions have even been established to protect the trade.

Judging from the popularity of the pendulum in so many of the new "adult" games available today, one might think of the whole concept as being primarily fun with a little luck thrown in. Not so. Far from being a simple and harmless practice, dowsing and pendulum use often result in serious mental and psychic disturbances. Case after case of such spiritual ill effects can be found in Dr. Kurt Koch's lengthy and rather technical treatise entitled, *"Seelsorge and Okkultismus" (Christian Counseling and Occultism.*[10]

A continual use of the divining rod or pendulum,

it has been proven, can produce serious psychic sicknesses not only for the user but for those who frequent such a person for advice or healing. Such an inquirer is usually led into a further pursuit of the occult through other means such as those already mentioned.

Mirrors

Mirror mantic is still another in the list of ancient fortune-telling practices. With the use of crystal balls, mirrors, rock crystal and still water, the gazer can be found uncovering crimes, finding hidden objects or diagnosing difficult diseases. (He is not to be confused with the mirror magician, who uses his power to heal, maim or persecute another person over great distances through the use of a mirror or other reflective device.)

In the months before he fatally wounded Robert F. Kennedy, Sirhan Sirhan steeped himself in the lore of occultism—primarily that of mirror mantic. In an article titled "Sirhan Through the Looking Glass," *Time* magazine reported: "A mirror. Two flickering candles. And Sirhan Sirhan. Alone in his cramped room, day after day, hour after silent hour, Sirhan studied Sirhan. . . .

"Focusing his mind power on the looking glass, Sirhan soon convinced himself that he could order an inanimate object to move. He rigged a pendulum from a fisherman's weight, and on command, he said, it began to sway. Yet *telekinesis*—the ability to cause objects at a distance to move through the exercise of will—was a frightening power, and

Sirhan feared that he might lose his mind. Once, instead of his own image in the mirror, Sirhan saw a vision of Robert Kennedy, the man he was soon afterward to kill."[11]

In reviewing the case, the psychoanalyst, Dr. Bernard L. Diamond, noted, "One key to the killing must be found in Sirhan's arcane experiments with the mirror. It was during his self-induced trances that Sirhan scribbled over and over 'Kennedy must die!' "[12]

I have mentioned only a few of the various practices of fortune-telling: astrology, cartomancy, palmistry, numerology, rod and pendulum and mirror mantic. The discussion could be carried further to include the reading of tea leaves, coffee grounds, beetle crawlings and plant growth if we wished to do so. Suffice it to say that the principle is basically the same in each.

The same pattern seems to be present in all of the forms of fortune-telling. At first the seeker is usually critical of the accuracy of any of the mantic practices. When he does open himself up to any one of the different fields of mantic, he finds too much truth to toss out the whole thing. Usually just about the same conclusion is reached whether one is told his horoscope by an astrologer or has his future revealed by a palmist or card layer. And then, before he knows it, the skeptic is a full-fledged believer and advocate of the ancient crafts.

As in every case of authentic fortune-telling, the autosuggestion or auto-hypnosis exercized by the clairvoyant definitely operates in the subconscious area of the mind. Being out of the control of the conscious mind, the subconscious can be influenced not only by past experience but also by outer-human forces.

In his book, *The Realities of Religious Experience*, William James says that "our normal waking consciousness . . . is but one special type of consciousness: whilst all about it, parted from it by the filmiest of screens, there lie potential forms of consciousness entirely different. . . . No account of the universe in its totality can be final which leaves these other forms of consciousness quite disregarded." And the existence of these forms, James continues, "forbids a premature closing of our accounts with reality."[13]

This is one of the primary reasons for the apostle Paul's warning that we do not wrestle against flesh and blood—but against the evil spirits of the air.[14]

One of the main reasons for the sudden popularity of the fortune-telling arts is a reaction to an over-emphasis upon the mental—the thinking, rational part of man—and a corresponding suppression of that which is emotional, mystical or supernatural. We have been taught that scientific intellectualism offers prime keys to understanding the universe. Chiefly because of this emphasis, we have put empirical knowledge on the pinnacle of our search for meaning.

Then we have seen many of those who have reached the top come down empty, tired and bitter. Universities have left behind their original belief in a Creator God and have turned instead to worshiping and serving His creation. Many churches have removed every element of the supernatural from their creeds, have watered down the teachings of Scripture as merely good moral principles for successful living and have emphasized social programs at the expense of spiritual truth. And the result of this has been futility.

The alternative

Little wonder we are so vulnerable today to occultism. By reacting against science, we have run to the opposite extreme of meaninglessness and fatalism. If our life is programmed when we are born, there is no place for living and being human—no joy, no sorrow—only a stoic attitude of indifference to the inevitable.

The existentialist philosophy which has become so popular in the twentieth century says that life indeed has no meaning. It is all a game in which everyone who is born eventually loses. In a world that has become so pessimistic, so fatalistic, so afraid of its own shadow, there is little which inspires our faith. And the nature of man is that he must have faith in *something* more powerful and stable than himself in order to survive. Along come the card layers, the magicians, the tea-leaf readers with their promises of power and insight into life. What modern-day man, backed against the wall with his very soul at stake, could ignore the temptations of the occult? And so once again man begins to place his faith in something beyond himself and his minuscule finite world.

Faith, you see, is the central issue. There is the faith of a few that man will progress and perfect himself on his own, without the help of God. But faith in human progress is folly. On the other hand, there are those who say that "all is vanity," that things are the way they are and nothing can be done to change or improve them. This philosophy of faith in fatalism is also folly.

There is a faith, however, that stands between folly and fatalism. The faith of which I speak is not groundless "blind faith," but is based upon totally rational, reasonable premises.

This faith is revealed to us in the Word of God.

The apostle Paul wrote to the church at Rome and reminded them that that which is known about God is evident (i.e., His eternal power and divine nature) and can be clearly understood through what has been created in nature and the heavens. But "even though they knew God, they did not honor Him as God, or give thanks; but they became futile in their speculations, and their foolish heart was darkened. Professing themselves to be wise, they became fools."[15]

Here lies the problem: God has revealed Himself to man through the beauty and perfection of nature, through the stars which serve as "signs" and "witnesses" to the Creator and His plan of redemption, and through human life which reveals a part of the mind and heart of God. But man rebels against the thought that he is less than God. So he looks to every seemingly feasible explanation for life except the craftsmanship of an all-wise, all-knowing yet profoundly personal God.

Having shut his mind to the idea of a personal God, man must look to spiritists, clairvoyants and astrologers to find meaning in life. ". . . when you did not know God," Paul writes to the Christians at Galatia, "you were slaves to these which by nature are no gods," and further refers to their former slavery to "the weak and worthless elemental things. . . ."[16]

Paul uses the term "elemental spirits" (Greek, *stoicheia*) or the basic elements of the world. The same *fire, earth, air* and *water* that the alchemists of old believed were what creation could be reduced to, could very well have been in the back of Paul's mind at the time. It seems that men are not content to be humbled by an almighty God who loves them and wants their companionship. This has always been the reason for man's attempts to create God in his image—like idols of men and animals made from wood and clay.[17]

Though God is a God of love, He is also a God of justice. And He will not let man play God. Any attempt at fortune-telling, for this reason, is a violation of the first and greatest commandment given by God to man, "Thou shalt have no other gods before me." God does not tolerate idolatry—and the worship of any other being or thing than almighty God is punishable by God's judgment.

God knew that mantic is an inferior path to wisdom and knowledge. It is for this reason that He spoke through Moses saying, "The person who turns to mediums and to spiritists, to play the harlot after them, I will set My face against that person and will cut him off from among his people."[18]

The penalty, in fact, for being an astrologer or fortune-teller in Old Testament times was death by stoning.[19] The book of Deuteronomy tells us that "there shall not be found among you anyone who makes his son or his daughter pass through the fire, one who uses divination, one who practices witchcraft, or one who interprets omens, or a sorcerer, or one who casts a spell, or a medium, or a spiritist, or one who calls up the dead. For whoever does these things is detestable to the Lord."[20]

Later in history, God pronounced judgment on His people Israel through the prophet Isaiah:

"But evil will come on you
Which you will not know how to charm away;
And disaster will fall on you
For which you cannot atone,
And destruction about which you do not know
Will come on you suddenly.
Stand fast now in your spells
And in your many sorceries
With which you have labored from your youth;
Perhaps you will be able to profit,
Perhaps you may cause trembling.
You are wearied with your many counsels,
Let now the astrologers,
Those who prophesy by the stars,
Those who predict by the new moons,
Stand up and save you from what will come upon you.
Behold, they have become like stubble,
Fire burns them;
They cannot deliver themselves from the power of the flame;
There will be no coal to warm by,
Nor a fire to sit before!

So have those become to you with whom you
have labored,
Who have trafficked with you from your youth;
Each has wandered in his own way.
There is none to save you."[21]

The third reason for God's displeasure with fortune-telling is found in the very need for a fortune-teller. In every case of mantic, a person or object is used as a "go-between." The prediction does not come through direct contact with God but always through a mediator.

But the Scriptures tell us that "there is one God, and *one mediator* also between God and men, the man Christ Jesus, who gave Himself as a ransom for all."[22]

God's evaluation

Here, then, are the three main reasons why fortune-telling is contrary to the person and teachings of God:

First of all, it is a violation of the first commandment given by God to man: no other god or gods are to be worshiped in place of the only true God who created the heavens and the earth and *all* that is in them, including man.

Secondly, fortune-telling is an inferior form of wisdom and knowledge. God alone is the true source of insight into the world around us and our own nature and future.

Thirdly, the New Testament teaches that Jesus Christ came to earth to be the mediator between God and man once and for all. Fortune-telling is an attempt to usurp His role as man's mediator to God by using devices and people instead of the power and presence of Christ.

But what about the results of fortune-telling? Haven't many of the predictions of these readings come about?

A good question—yes, many forecasts have been highly accurate. The apostle John, however, tells us that we should not believe every spirit but should test the spirits to see whether they are from God: "because many false prophets have gone out into the world."[23]

Paul and his traveling companion Silas encountered one such counterfeit fortune-teller during their travels in the city of Philippi.[24] While walking the busy street toward the temple, they were confronted by a slave girl who kept shouting, "These men are bond-servants of the Most High God, who are proclaiming to you the way of salvation." The incident repeated itself day after day until the girl's shouting became more of an attraction than Paul's preaching about Jesus. Finally he commanded the spirit, "In the name of Jesus Christ to come out of her!"[25] Paul had realized the existence of an evil spirit in the girl and had cast it out by the power of God to the anger of the syndicate that owned her and, we are told, were doing quite well by the fortune-telling profits she was bringing them. This act, which cost Paul and Silas imprisonment and severe beatings, is biblical testimony to the fact that correct and true predictions can be made by one who is under the control of a spirit which totally opposes

God. "All that glitters is not gold," as the old expression so aptly expresses it.

If what the fortune-tellers predict often comes true, how much more, then, will God's predictions concerning those who both practice and use fortune-telling be fulfilled? God has promised in His Word that those who are involved in these practices will one day face His wrath and His judgment.

"If any of you lacks wisdom," James tells the Christians in his letter to them, "let him ask of God, who gives to all men generously . . . and it will be given to him."[26] Not "ask a fortune-teller," not "ask an astrologer," not "ask the Tarot cards." ASK GOD!

What better fortune could a person have than the one promised to all believers in Jesus Christ, "And we know that God causes all things to work together for good to those who love God, to those who are called according to His purpose."[27]

Footnotes for Chapter 5

1. "Papus" (Dr. Gerard Encausse), a leading French occultist, is quoted as saying: "The gypsy . . . has given us the key which enables us to explain all the symbolism of the ages . . . . In it, where a man of the people sees only the key to an obscure tradition, (are) discovered the mysterious links which unite God, the Universe, and Man." (*The Tarot of the Bohemians,* New York: Arcanum Books, 1889.)

2. The "minor arcana" is comprised of 56 cards, the "major arcana" of 22. *Arcana* is the Latin word for "secrets."

3. Eden Gray, *The Tarot Revealed* (New York: Inspiration House, 1960), p. 3.

4. Kurt Koch, D.D., *Between Christ and Satan* (Berghausan BD. Germany, Evangelization Publishers, 1961), p. 14. U.S. edition: Grand Rapids: Kregel Publications, 1968.

5. Gray, *The Tarot Revealed,* p. 117.

6. "Jehovah" was abbreviated in the Hebrew by eliminating the vowels, thus allowing the name to be referred to as "Y-H-W-H." (Pistis Sophia wrote in the third century, A.D., "Nothing therefore is more excellent than the mysteries which ye seek after, saving only the mystery of the Seven Vowels and their forty and nine Powers, and the numbers thereof. And no name is as excellent as all these [vowels] . . .")

7. J. Walton-Jordan in "Your Number and Destiny," *Man, Myth and Magic* (Great Britain: Purnell, Inc., 1970), vol. 1, no. 2, p. 69. Italics added.

8. For further elaboration see chapters 2 and 3 of Richard Cavendish's *The Black Arts* (New York: G.P. Putnam & Sons, 1967), or R. Cavendish, "Alphabet," *Man, Myth and Magic,* vol. 1, no. 1, pp. 69-72.

9. For further reading E. W. Bullinger, *Number in Scripture* (Grand Rapids: Kregel Publications, 1967). Reproduced from original edition of 1894.

10. Kurt E. Koch, *Seelsorge und Okkultismus* (Grand Rapids: Kregel Publications, 1965), pp. 81-93.

11. "Sirhan Through the Looking Glass," *Time,* April 4, 1969, p. 28.

12. "Sirhan Through the Looking Glass."

13. McCandlish Phillips, *The Bible, the Supernatural and the Jews* (New York and Cleveland: The World Publishing Co., 1970), p. 237.

14. Ephesians 6:12.

15. Romans 1:21,22.

16. Galatians 4:8,9.

17. Romans 1.

18. Leviticus 20:6.

19. Leviticus 20:27.

20. Deuteronomy 18:10-12.

21. Isaiah 47:11-15.

22. 1 Timothy 2:5,6.

23. 1 John 4:1.

24. Acts 16:16-21.

25. Acts 16:18.

26. James 1:5.

27. Romans 8:28.

> *"Russia will be the first nation to put a man on the moon, probably in about three years' time."*

Jeane Dixon
A Gift of Prophecy

CHAPTER 6

On Saying Sooth

"I see you in a hospital with arms and legs raised as though in a cast," the mystic told Sacramento TV personality Harry Martin during a television interview on September 29, 1971.[1]

Martin was skeptical. Perhaps the mystic, Mary Lou Smith, had mistakenly seen Martin's hospitalized wife in her vision. It was certainly not him. Or so he thought.

Five hours later Martin reasoned differently as he lay in a hospital bed with his left leg raised in a cast to protect his newly-broken ankle. The auto accident a few hours before had somewhat changed his mind about prophets.

So Harry Martin added his name to the rapidly

growing list of believers in the art of prophecy—a list headed by many sincerely religious people as well as thousands of nonreligious enthusiasts.

Prophecy is no new thing. Four thousand years ago Babylonian kings thought it a solemn and infallible ritual to have an animal's liver extracted and "read" for them by a professional seer. The condition of the organ, the number of convolutions, and the arrangement of the blood vessels determined the dates and results of future wars and kingdoms overthrown. The liver at that time was believed to be the seat of one's life and existence, much as the brain and heart are known to be today.

A true reading was expected every time. A false one often cost the seer his life.

We have the same thing today with two minor exceptions. First of all, our "modern" methodology has replaced animal entrails with crystal balls, visions and dreams. Secondly, the penalty for error is considerably less drastic—a necessary leniency to preserve the survival of the trade. The methods and modes of prophecy may have become varied over the centuries, but visions, dreams and prophetic utterances are as current as the daily newspaper and as commonplace as the morning sunrise.

For many present-day seers, prophecy is a well-paying game. Capitalizing on the "humanness" of man and his desire for knowledge and power, the mystics promise a way out of the confines of today into the boundless dimensions of the future.

Criswell, the Liberace of popular prophecy, has become a byword for entertaining predictions. His appearances on nationwide variety and talk shows prove the popularity and mass appeal of prophecy. Relying on known facts and trends, the mighty Criswell projects the probable outcome of a given situation, embellishes it with his self-conscious humor and serves it with the hackneyed preface, "I predict that . . ."

Yet, for all his flamboyance, Criswell still manages to intrigue, if not alarm, thousands of gullible Americans. As he puts it, "We are all interested in the future, for the future is where we will spend the rest of our lives."

Criswell is only one of many prophets who dot our daily lives. Who has not heard of Jeane Dixon? And Edgar Cayce, the "sleeping prophet," continues to haunt the American scene several decades after his passing. Merlin the magician is still alive in the imaginations of many today. Fableized in nineteenth century fairy tales as a King Arthur-type myth, Merlin did actually exist (in A.D. 415) several hundred years prior to Arthur's time and is reported to have made as many long-range predictions as his notable predecessor Nostradamus.

History texts are filled with the prophecies of famous seers as well as, in many cases, the fulfillment of same. Despite continual attacks against its authenticity and accuracy, prognostication continues to increase in popularity as it has throughout history. Each generation of humans has had its own peculiar prophet or prophetess.

Of special interest to many today who follow "popular" prophecy is the name Jeane Dixon.

Most people by now are at least partially aware of the impact Mrs. Dixon has had upon the national and international affairs of the past two decades. The prophecies of this Wisconsin-born seeress have been well documented in her two books, *A Gift of Prophecy*[2] and *My Life and Prophecies*,[3] along with countless magazine, newspaper, and television reports of her prognostications.

The opinion in most circles today about Jeane Dixon is that she is a kind, sincere humanitarian with a deep faith in God, the Bible and the church. In addition to this, it is believed that she demonstrates a God-given gift of prophecy. As Jerome Ellison puts it, "She is probably about the nearest thing to an authentic but untypical Old Testament-style prophet our generation of Americans is likely to see."[4]

Because many people equate her with the biblical concept of a prophet, and because Mrs. Dixon herself claims to be a spokesman for God, it is important that we look deeper into her prophecies to see if they coincide with biblical teachings. If she is a true voice for God, then America in general and Christians in particular should take heed of her warnings. If, though, she is not a true representative of God, we should be quick to recognize this and denounce her as such.

May I suggest in the outset that we are dealing with two separate topics. The first is the person of Jeane Dixon; the second, her proclamations. We shall endeavor not to confuse the two.

Mrs. Dixon's observable personal life is of the highest caliber—a fine example of selflessness and kindness to others. Her record of years of volunteer service to needy charities and repeated compassion for the poor and underprivileged is most praiseworthy. Her personal interest in children of all ages and backgrounds has established her as one of the great humanitarians of our day. The poor, the black, the immigrant, the unwed mother, the troubled teenager—each considers Mrs. Dixon a friend. And rightly so.

Her marriage to Mr. James Dixon seems to be an example of harmony and love. Each night, without fail, her husband places a fresh rose on her pillow. If he is out of town, he has one delivered to her.

Jeane is also a very dedicated churchwoman. She attends Mass daily, as she has done regularly all her life. She begins each day by standing at her bedroom window, facing east and repeating the Twenty-Third Psalm. She ends each day with a time of introspection and meditation before God.

One of the most outstanding things one notices about Mrs. Dixon is that she never accepts remuneration for her advice and counsel. Her gift of prophecy, she believes, was given to her by God and could easily be taken from her were she to misuse it for her own gain.

Jeane Dixon is truly a remarkable woman—intelligent, sensitive, charitable and sincere.

Acknowledging this, however, we must be careful not to judge a person's veracity by his character alone. Jeane Dixon's proclamations must be judged in light of the truth of Scripture, not merely by her personal actions. "I have been given certain psychic gifts which I have been working to develop and use in accordance with God's will as I am able to understand His will—His purpose for my life," Mrs. Dixon states in her book, *My Life and Prophecies.*[5] Are these gifts of prediction really from God? Is Jeane Dixon really God-inspired when she sees her visions? Is she really, like the prophets of the Old Testament, God's spokesman to mankind?

It is the opinion of this author that she is *not.* Whatever else she may be, Jeane Dixon does not pass the biblical test of a true prophet inspired by the God of the Bible. The following facts are important considerations in weighing the evidence.

1. *Many of her prophecies are so general and vaguely lacking in detail that any number of interpretations could be made from them.*

Prophecies such as the continued split in matters of dogma within the Catholic church[6] and increased concern over student unrest[7] are typical of such elusive predictions. Often her prophecies are mere extensions of already existing situations or probably results of already known plans. Such "predictions" are often embellished to make them popular to large segments of the general populace.

2. *She makes a disturbing distinction between "revelation" and "telepathy."*[8]

Although Mrs. Dixon believes that certain profound revelations of God's will have been given her, she maintains that these are few and far between. "Sometimes two, three or even four years may go by without God granting me a revelation," she says, "and then some morning I wake up and feel just wonderful. I feel inspired and know something great is going to happen."[9]

The pattern of these "God-given revelations" is as follows: *First-through-third day*—a building sense of love and peace. "I have that spring in my walk that I do not usually have." *Fourth day*—the anticipated revelation in the form of a dream or a vision. *Fifth-through-seventh day*—a continued sense of love and peace.[10] Typical of these revelations was the predicted assassination of President John F. Kennedy, which came to her in 1956, four years before his election and eleven years before the Dallas tragedy. These "revelations," according to Mrs. Dixon, are exact and cannot be altered by men or circumstances.

"Telepathic predictions," on the other hand, are only vibrations of human intent and can be changed if people so wish. The deaths of Dr. Martin Luther King, Jr., and Senator Robert F. Kennedy were revealed to Mrs. Dixon prior to their occurrence through mental telepathy. The circumstances could have been changed, she reports, and the destinies of these men altered for the good.[11]

In addition to this questionable distinction between "revelation" and "telepathy," she finds it necessary to make allowances for error. "When a psychic vision is not fulfilled as expected," she cautions, "it is not because what has been shown me is not correct; *it is because I have not interpreted the symbols correctly.*"[12]

Couple this allowance for error with a hazy differentiation between permanent revelations and changeable telepathy and you end up with a rather easy cop-out for wrong predictions. (This "out" would have saved the lives of many prophets who

89

falsely prophesied in the Old Testament and were executed for their error.)

3. *Many of Jeane Dixon's predictions have proven wrong and are therefore false prophecies.*

Since many of her prophecies were communicated orally in private talks, there is no way to substantiate their authenticity except by the testimony of those involved. For that reason, we cannot speak of any predictions prior to 1952 (when Mrs. Ruth Montgomery began writing her famous column on Jeane Dixon) or any predictions which were not made public at the time of their utterance. But those that have been written about offer printed proof of her inaccuracy.

Though Jeane correctly guessed the death of Franklin D. Roosevelt in 1945[13] and the assassination of Mahatma Gandhi in 1948,[14] she failed in her prediction that Lyndon Johnson would receive the 1968 presidential nomination from the Democratic party when that nomination went to Hubert Humphrey.[15] She failed again by declaring on the very day before the Jackie Kennedy-Aristotle Onassis wedding that Jackie had no thoughts of marriage.[16] Again, though she correctly predicted the re-election of President Harry Truman and was even correct about his rival nominee, Thomas E. Dewey,[17] she also predicted that Red China would plunge into war over Quemoy and Matsu in October of 1958.[18] Of course, the latter encounter never occurred.

While prophecies regarding the death of Chief Justice Fred Vinson and a merger of the A.F.L. and

C.I.O. unions were fulfilled,[19] a prophecy that Walter Reuther would actively seek the presidency in 1964 was way "off target."[20] According to Mrs. Dixon, he was to receive the Democratic nomination and Richard Nixon was to oppose him on the Republican ticket. History records that Reuther did not even seek the presidency in 1964, let alone receive the Democratic nomination. Furthermore, Richard Nixon did not receive the Republican nomination that year.[21]

On the positive side, she correctly picked "Native Dancer" to come in second in the 1953 Kentucky Derby;[22] but negatively, she predicted that World War III would break out in 1958.[23] Needless to say, whatever else that year saw, it did not see World War III!

Ruth Montgomery claims that Jeane Dixon foresaw several heart attacks for President Dwight Eisenhower in 1955 and his re-election in November of 1956,[24] both of which occurred as predicted. Jeane also predicted on January 1, 1953 that President Eisenhower would soon appoint General Douglas MacArthur to a very important post in his administration, probably an ambassadorship.[25] (The historical record reveals that such an appointment never occurred.)

The death of Jawaharlal Nehru was predicted in 1956 to take place seven years later.[26] In May of 1964, Nehru died. On December 28, 1958 Mrs. Dixon forecasted the death of Secretary of State John Foster Dulles by the middle of the following year.[27] By the end of May, 1959, Dulles was dead. In the same way, she foresaw the plane crash which would take the life of Dag Hammarskold three years after her vision.[28] Sir Winston Churchill's death in 1964 was predicted[29] as well as Edward Kennedy's plane crash which occurred the day after she made her prediction.[30] In addition, the suicide of Marilyn Monroe[31] and the Alaskan earthquake[32] were both predicted by Jeane Dixon prior to their occurrences.

But, on the other hand, Mrs. Dixon was totally wrong in predicting the following events: 1) Red China's admission to the United Nations in 1959;[33] 2) the Conservative Party's victory in England's 1964 election;[34] 3) Russia and China's rule by a "swarthy skinned man who was part Oriental" by 1964;[35] 4) the end of the Vietnam War ninety days from her prophecy on May 7, 1966;[36] 5) peace negotiations on Vietnam early in 1966;[37] 6) the creation of a new U.S. administrative position of "assistant President" and a rivalry between Dewey and Senator William Knowland for this spot;[38] 7) the immediate improvement in U.S. relations with France and French President Charles de Gaulle as a result of President Johnson's appointment of a new ambassador to France.[39]

Added to the above list of false prophecies should be her forecast regarding the late Bishop James Pike. In her book, *My Life and Prophecies* published in September of 1969, she forsees the Bishop leaving the clergy and becoming a man of genius such as a "medical diagnostician."[40] Strangely enough, the very month her book was published Bishop Pike's body was found by Bedouins and police officials on the Israeli desert surrounding the

Red Sea.[41] "Fortunately," Dixon says of him in her book, "I see that he will lose his frustration in his new vocation."[42]

I have mentioned only a few of Jeane Dixon's erroneous prophecies to illustrate a point. The Old Testament states with authority that when a prophet is truly speaking in the name of the Lord, *what he says must come true.*[43] If what he prophesies does not come true, he is not representing the Lord.[44] Thus, we can see that a true prophet of God makes predictions that are not hit and miss, as in the case of Mrs. Dixon. They either must all come true or we have the biblical testimony that the person is not a prophet of God.[45]

A true prophecy originates from God and is therefore pure. A true prophet will be able to relay this message in its pure form without needing to make allowance for error. Throughout the Old Testament, we read prophecies prefaced with "The Word of the Lord came to Zechariah,"[46] or "The Lord spoke again to Moses,"[47] or "Thus says the Lord."[48] When God speaks through one of His prophets, there is no doubt as to whether that prophecy will take place—it will.

4. A true prophet of God speaks primarily to the sins of men and about the judgment of God—subjects rarely referred to by Jeane Dixon.

Throughout the Scriptures, the central message of God's prophets was not directed toward improving Israel's relations with other nations but with revealing the transgressions of God's people and His resultant judgment.[49]

A pronouncement as "This year we will make tremendous overall progress, moving in the right direction as the President gains strength in his second year"[50] is almost humorous when compared to the mighty declarations of God's holiness and justice and man's sinfulness in the Old and New Testaments. There has never been a prophet of God who spoke of anything else but God, His workings among men and His desire for man to repent and come into a relationship with Himself. I challenge you to find a prophet in the Bible who spoke otherwise.

If Jeane Dixon were to speak for the God she claims to represent, she would speak judgment to those who have forsaken Him.[51] There appears to be very little mention in any of her writings of the fact of sin and the finality of life without God. She completely overlooks the biblical teaching that after death there is the certainty of eternal separation from God unless one has exercised repentance toward God and faith in Jesus Christ.[52]

5. *Many of the methods used by Jeane Dixon are forbidden by God in the Scriptures.*

One of Mrs. Dixon's first indications of her psychic gift came through a nomadic gypsy woman who visited her when she was only eight years old. The woman declared that never before had she seen palm lines like Jeane's. In her left hand was the Star of David with double lines leading from it, and in the right, there was another star on the Mount of Jupiter. The gypsy declared that Jean Pinckert (Jeane's maiden name) was blessed with the gift of prophecy and that she would foresee worldwide changes—a prediction later verified by a Hindu mystic.[53]

The gypsy gave young Jeane a crystal ball in which the girl immediately saw the gypsy with burned and bandaged hands. When the gypsy woman left the room and then returned, her hands were bandaged, as Jeane had predicted. The crystal ball, along with an incomplete deck of cards, were the first of Jeane Dixon's collection of occult devices.[54]

In addition to cards and the crystal ball, Mrs. Dixon makes use of horoscopes and numerology, practices which are condemned throughout the Bible[55] (See chapter 4 of this book for a more detailed discussion of such occult devices.)

6. *Jeane Dixon does not meet biblical standards for a prophet (or prophetess) of God.*

Rene Noorbergen, Mrs. Dixon's latest associate, writes in Jeane's book *My Life and Prophecies* that it is only God's Spirit working through Mrs. Dixon who is responsible for her visions and prophecies.[56] Mrs. Noorbergen then goes on to list several biblical "tests" of a true prophet. Consider some of these with me.

(A) "Under what influence did the prophets of old speak?"

Her answer: "For no prophecy was ever made by an act of human will, but men moved by the Holy Spirit spoke from God."[57]

Consider: the Bible teaches that prophecy comes not by the will of man but by God's Spirit. Why,

95

then, are there so many flagrant errors in Mrs. Dixon's predictions? Has the Spirit of God made mistakes—or is Mrs. Dixon relying on her own power rather than the power of God? Why haven't her predictions come about as foretold in the same way that the God's Old Testament prophets were invariably right?

(B) "By what means has God generally made known His will to man?"

Her answer: "I have also spoken to the prophets, and I gave numerous visions; and through the prophets I gave parables."[58]

Consider: there is also reference in Noorbergen's answer at this point to Hebrews 1:1,2, but the verses are not printed. Listen to them: "God, after He spoke long ago to the fathers in the prophets in many portions and in many ways, in these last days has spoken to us in His Son. . . ." This contradicts her entire premise. In Old Testament times, God spoke through His prophets, but today He speaks through the message which Jesus Christ brought to mankind. Our knowledge of what Jesus Christ has already spoken is the Word of God.

(C) "What test should be applied in determining the validity of a person's claim to be a prophet?"

Her answer: "If a prophet or a dreamer of dreams arises among you and gives you a sign or a wonder, and the sign or the wonder comes true, concerning which he spoke to you, saying, 'Let us go after other gods (whom you have not known) and let us serve them,' you shall not listen to the words of that prophet or that dreamer of dreams; for the Lord your God is testing you to find out if you love the

Lord your God with all your heart and with all your soul. You shall follow the Lord your God and fear Him; and you shall keep His commandments, listen to His voice, serve Him, and cling to Him."[59]

Consider: the very Scripture which is quoted by Rene Noorbergen teaches that we should keep God's commandments. One of His commandments is Deuteronomy 18:9-12, which forbids the use of tools such as crystal balls and cards.

(D) "What rule did Christ give for distinguishing between true and false prophets?"

Her answer: "So then, you will know them by their fruits."[60]

Consider: Exactly! And, as the apostle James puts it, a fountain does not gush forth both fresh and bitter water.[61] If the fruit is sometimes good and at other times bad, as in the case of Jeane Dixon's prophecies, the tree cannot be trusted.

(E) "Are prophets called to minister to the church primarily or to non-Christians?"

Her answer: "One who prophesies edifies the church."[62]

Consider: again, Jeane Dixon's prophecies are for the world in general and the United States in particular. None of her prophecies apply only to the church of Christ (that is, those who have placed personal faith in Jesus Christ as the Son of God). None!

(F) "What general rule is laid down for testing all prophets?"

Her answer: "To the law and to the testimony: if they speak not according to this word, it is because there is no light in them."[63]

Consider: in her latest book, Mrs. Dixon summarizes her teaching by saying that "from the sum of many lives being led apart from God's purposes comes the turmoil and destruction of riots, revolutions and wars among nations," as well as individual unrest, unhappiness and broken lives. Her answer is that we must all "begin to function as a team with each one of us fulfilling his important purpose."[64]

Teamwork will accomplish nothing unless there is a team in the first place. The message of the "Law and the Testimony" of the Word of God is not that mankind form a team that can work together but that men be reconciled to a just and loving God through faith in His only Son.[65]

Jeane Dixon speaks not "according to the law and testimony." Isaiah's conclusion is indisputable.

7. *The final consideration as to the veracity of Jeane Dixon as a prophet of God is that she does not proclaim Jesus Christ to be the only way one can personally know God.*[66]

It is clear from reading Jeane Dixon's books that her belief in God is built around the humanistic idea of the "brotherhood of man" under the "fatherhood of God."[67] But the Bible teaches that God is Father only to those who have personally trusted Jesus Christ.

When Jeane Dixon speaks of the will of God for each person's life, she believes that knowing this will and being in it are based upon developing our talents as humans. By using our talents to their fullest potential, we can know God personally. She says, "And to diminish that which we alone in the world possess is to reject the will of God."[68] But Scripture teaches that the will of God is something other than human talent development. "For this is the will of My Father, that every one who beholds the Son, and believes in Him, may have eternal life."[69]

Jeane Dixon states that it is "Only when we recognize and accept life as a unique gift, a *special* gift, and employ our individual talents to the fullest measure of our capabilities will we find harmony within ourselves, with Him and the universe. It is this balance within that determines our stature among men and before God."[70] Nowhere in Scripture can this idea be found—in fact the opposite runs throughout all of the teachings of both Jesus and Paul. Paul tells us that *nothing* which we possess can put us in good standing with a holy and righteous God—not our talents or our good wishes or our desire to be good people.[71] The only thing which puts us into fellowship with God is believing in His Son, Jesus Christ.

The apostle Peter states unequivocally that "there is salvation in no one else; for there is no other name under heaven that has been given among men, by which we must be saved."[72]

Not only does Jeane Dixon not proclaim Jesus Christ as the only way to God—she rarely speaks of Him at all!

Summarizing the foregoing considerations I would suggest the following. Based on the evaluation of the claims and prophecies of Jeane Dixon in the light of the standards presented in the Word of God, there is no alternative but to expose her as a false prophet. The apostle John warns Christians that they should "not believe every spirit, but test the spirits to see whether they are from God; because many false prophets have gone out into the world."[13]

Not every one who prophesies in the name of the Lord speaks for God. The Lord Jesus spoke these words, "Many will say to Me on that day, 'Lord, Lord, did we not prophesy in Your name? . . .' And then will I declare to them, 'I never knew you; depart from Me, you who practice lawlessness.' "[14]

As Russell T. Hitt (editor of *Eternity* magazine) has said, the very fact that she is so popular among Christians is a reflection of the lamentable state of the believing church. There is only one prophetic message which Christians need to be concerned about: that Jesus is returning soon to claim His own and set up His kingdom on earth. This is where Bible prophecy ultimately points.

We are living in a time when false prophets appear on the scene each and every day. Christ Himself warned us of such occurrences when He said, "And then if anyone says to you, 'Behold, here is the Christ;' or 'Behold, He is there;' do not believe him; for false Christs and false prophets will arise, and will show signs and wonders, in order, if possible, to lead the elect astray. But take heed; behold, I have told you everything in advance."[15]

When a seemingly prophetic voice utters anything other than Jesus Christ and His salvation and power, we must take heed of Jesus' clear warnings.

What, then, can be said in summary of Jeane Dixon? That she is a woman with an amazing power of prediction and a heightened sense of ESP and telepathy? Yes. That she is a humanitarian who wishes very deeply for a world of peace and brotherly love? Yes. That she is a modern-day prophet of God who speaks His message in a world which cries out for a soul-changing answer to life's problems? Definitely NO!

Her voice may be the voice of intelligence, of sound reasoning and of humanitarian appeal, but it is not the voice of God.

In his Second Epistle, the apostle Peter vividly recalls to mind his experience on the mountain with James, John and Jesus.[16] As though it were happening all over again, he sees before him the brilliance of the transfiguration of the Son of God and the sudden appearance of Moses and the prophet Elijah. Then, as Peter begins to interrupt their conversation, a bright cloud overshadows them and a voice thunders out of the heavens saying:

"This is My beloved Son with whom I am well pleased." HEAR HIM!

The tragedy today is that most people are listening to the wrong voices.

"If a blind man guides a blind man," Jesus said, "both will fall into a pit."[17]

Footnotes for Chapter 6

1. *Los Angeles Times,* Oct. 1, 1971.

2. Ruth A. Montgomery, *A Gift of Prophecy* (New York: Bantam Books, 1966), 196 pp.

3. Jeane Dixon, *My Life and Prophecies* (New York: Bantam Books, 1970), 246 pp.

4. Jerome Ellison in *20th Century Prophecies* by James Bjornstad (Minneapolis: Bethany Fellowship, 1969), p. 14.

5. Dixon, *My Life and Prophecies,* p. 62.

6. Dixon, *My Life and Prophecies,* p.152.

7. Dixon, *My Life and Prophecies,* p. 154.

8. Dixon, *My Life and Prophecies,* pp. 58-61,116.

9. Dixon, *My Life and Prophecies,* p. 59.

10. Dixon, *My Life and Prophecies,* p. 59.

11. Dixon, *My Life and Prophecies,* pp. 60, 115.

12. Dixon, *My Life and Prophecies,* p. 102. Italics added.

13. *Montgomery, A Gift of Prophecy, pp.* 48, 51

14. Montgomery, *A Gift of Prophecy,* p. 76.

15. *The Herald News,* Jan. 27, 1968, p. 7.

16. *The Herald News,* Oct. 19, 1968, p. 1.

17. Montgomery, *A Gift of Prophecy,* p. 87.

18. Montgomery, *A Gift of Prophecy,* p. 175.

19. Montgomery, *A Gift of Prophecy,* p. 83.

20. Montgomery, *A Gift of Prophecy,* p. 176.

21. *Harper's,* June, 1967, p. 38. (Cf. Montgomery, *A Gift of Prophecy,* p. 109.)

22. Montgomery, *A Gift of Prophecy,* p. 96.

23. *Harper's,* June, 1967, p. 37.

24. Montgomery, *A Gift of Prophecy,* p. 103.

25. *New York Daily News,* January 1, 1953.

26. Montgomery, *A Gift of Prophecy,* p. 30.

27. Montgomery, *A Gift of Prophecy,* p. 83.

28. Montgomery, *A Gift of Prophecy,* p. 83.

29. Montgomery, *A Gift of Prophecy,* p. 101.

30. Montgomery, *A Gift of Prophecy,* p. 13.

31. Montgomery, *A Gift of Prophecy,* p. 81.

32. *The Christian Herald,* March, 1966, p. 41.

33. *Harper's,* June, 1967, p. 37.

34. *Harper's,* June, 1967, p. 38.

35. Martin Ebon, *Prophecy in Our Time* (New York: The New American Library, 1968), p. 195.

36. Ebon, *Prophecy in Our Time,* pp. 192-193.

37. Ebon, *Prophecy in Our Time,* p. 193.

38. Ebon, *Prophecy in Our Time,* pp. 195-196.

39. *Harper's,* June, 1967, p. 37.

40. Dixon, *My Life and Prophecies,* p. 165.

41. Merrill F. Unger, *The Haunting of Bishop Pike* (Wheaton: Tyndale House, 1971), p. 7.

42. Dixon, *My Life and Prophecies*, p. 165.

43. Deuteronomy 18:22. Italics added.

44. God cannot lie (Hebrews 6:18; Titus 1:2). 2 Peter 1:21, "For no prophecy was ever made by an act of human will, but men moved by the Holy Spirit spoke from God." Jeane Dixon could not possibly have been moved by the Holy Spirit if (and since) many of her prophecies have been unquestionably wrong. See Deuteronomy 4:19.

45. Read the story of Moses in Exodus 4:10-16 to see God's power and ability to speak through men.

46. Zechariah 7:8.

47. Leviticus 23:1.

48. Jeremiah 30:2.

49. See Isaiah 58:1; Ezekiel 22:2; 43:10; Micah 3:8.

50. Dixon, *My Life and Prophecies*, p. 246.

51. Isaiah 30:18, "The Lord is a God of justice; How blessed are those who long for Him."

52. See John 3:16,36; 1 John 5:12.

53. Montgomery, *A Gift of Prophecy*, pp. 15, 16.

54. Montgomery, *A Gift of Prophecy*, pp. 17, 23, 29.

55. Deuteronomy 18:9-12; 2 Kings 23:24.

56. Rene Noorbergen in *My Life and Prophecies* by Jeane Dixon, p. 6.

57. Dixon, *My Life and Prophecies*, pp. 6, 7. (2 Peter 1:21.)

58. Dixon, *My Life and Prophecies*, p. 7. (Hosea 12:10.)

59. Dixon, *My Life and Prophecies*, p. 8. (Deuteronomy 13:1-4.)

60. Dixon, *My Life and Prophecies*, p. 8. (Matthew 7:20.)

61. James 3:11.

62. Dixon, *My Life and Prophecies*, p. 8. (1 Corinthians 14:4.)

63. Dixon, *My Life and Prophecies*, p. 9. (Isaiah 8:20. KJV).

64. Dixon, *My Life and Prophecies*, p. 236.

65. 2 Corinthians 5:17-21.

66. Jeane Dixon has stated, "There is only one God, and only one faith, but there are innumerable channels and each must find the right one for him." In elaborating on this, she uses the following illustration. "A Buddhist· is going to recognize that one power. So let us forget about such terms as 'Interfaith.' Let everybody seek his own faith at one Central Source." (*Christian Herald*, March, 1966, "Jeane Dixon Talks About God" by Jerome Ellison, p. 42.)
Buddhists, on the whole, refuse to admit to a single, almighty God. Rather, they believe man can reach godlike stature through discipline and human effort. Jeane Dixon's reasoning that "all roads lead to Rome" is totally opposed to the biblical position that Jesus Christ is God's only way to Himself.

67. Dixon, *My Life and Prophecies*, p. 237.

68. Dixon, *My Life and Prophecies*, p. 210.

69. John 6:40.

70. Dixon, *My Life and Prophecies*, p. 210.

71. Titus 3:5; Ephesians 2:8,9.

72. Acts 4:12.

73. 1 John 4:1-3.

74. Matthew 7:22,23.

75. Mark 13:21-23.

76. 2 Peter 1:16-18.

77. Matthew 15:14.

PART THREE
MAGIC

"*Diana and her darling crew shall
pluck your fingers fine,
And lead you forth right pleasantly
to sup the honey wine.
To sup the honey wine, my loves,
and breathe the heavenly air,
And dance, as the young angels dance.
Ah, god that I were there!*"

A 16th century version of a hymn to Diana

CHAPTER 7

The Ghost of Witches Past

A 37-year-old Paris typist recently suffered severe burns when she covered herself with cleaning fluid and set it alight. Her only explanation to the police was, "The witches are chasing me!"' Though we do not know what caused the woman to act this way, we do know that the belief in witchcraft today is as real to many as the belief in fortune-tellers.

"The practice of witchcraft, dormant in this part of the world for several centuries to all but a few hard-core believers, is back 'in' again," attests the *New York Scene*. "Satanism, magic, witchcraft (black and white, depending on whether it is evil or kindly), spells, card readings, covens, all those old practices which used to get one burned in medieval Europe or hanged in Puritan America, are discussed as easily over lunch as the latest shoe sale at Bloomingdales' or the play at the Music Box last night."[2]

Witchcraft, in fact, is no longer the isolated practice of any particular sociological group. It has rapidly found its way into the educational institutions of America. New York University and U.C.L.A. head the list of scores of colleges and universities which feature regular curricula and extension classes in the fundamentals of witchcraft. The University of Alabama's new experimental college encourages, in their witchcraft course, a field trip to view the Black Mass as celebrated at a nearby church. Says the Director of Continuing Education at Scarboro Community College of his course on the occult, "It's overflowing right now. Students pay fifteen dollars for 10 two-hour sessions, and though we didn't start the course to make money, let me tell you that it can be a real money-maker!"[3]

Resurgence of witchcraft

All over our country—and the world—today, people are overtly practicing the religion of witchcraft. What was once considered a practice punishable by death has now become "the thing to do." What is really surprising is that the renewed interest in witchcraft seems most prevalent among the highly educated, especially in America. "We have really become progressive around here," brags the dean of one of America's leading Catholic universities. "A couple of hundred years ago we would have burned them at the stake. Twenty-five years ago I would have expelled them. Now we simply send them all to psychiatrists."[4] TV documentaries have declared that numerous college and university campuses in the U.S. boast their own witch—or witches.

The scene in America is close approaching that of Europe's recent witchcraft obsession. Ever since sorcery was allowed out from the English underground in 1951 by Parliament's repeal of the Old Witchcraft Act, witches and their covens have been permitted the right of open assembly and news media coverage. "Faithful" in Germany, France and Italy join England in this procession of paganism. French men and women alone spend an estimated $200 million a year on witches, sorcerers, seers and healers—buying love potions, virility spells and numerous other herbs and accouterments. Reports from Switzerland indicate that there is scarcely a village that does not have a medium or witch who casts spells or brews potions in the manner of their medieval predecessors.

Capitalizing on this new trend, an Essex County (England) Council education advisor recently opened a school for would-be witches at a cost of thirty shillings for six lessons. Teaching his students how to concoct love potions, how to control a person by bewitching a doll and how to deal with enemies, he stands amazed at the phenomenal response to his lectures, both numerically and financially.

The *London Times* recently carried this typical ad: "A witch of full powers urgently sought to lift a 73-year-old curse and help restore the fortunes of an afflicted nobleman. Employment genuinely offered." In the same vein, a north London witch recalls that "eighteen months ago there were probably not more than twenty-six hundred of us grouped in covens of thirteen around the country." Today, however, he guesses that there are at least ten thousand British people actively interested and in some way participating in witchcraft.

As you scan your daily newspapers, you will hardly miss a day in which some news item will inform you of witchcraft happenings somewhere in the world, maybe even right in your own city. While kids tune into the TV show "Bewitched," about a good witch who marries a mortal and their subsequent problems and joys, thousands of adults are tuning to the real thing—the religion of witchcraft.

A definite distinction must be made between the three different forms of witchcraft: white, neutral and black magic. The three are not the same, even though the uninitiated would speak of them as being so.

Black magic (or "Satanism") usually admits to two separate deities, Good and Evil. For lack of satisfaction with the good deity, those involved in black magic worship his opposite; the majority of those involved in black magic actually worship Satan.

Those who practice neutral magic regard it as a much purer system. They believe that there is one god (or force) who can take on the form of good or evil depending upon the desire of his worshipers and the nature of the requested petition. Since the deity in this case is controlled, if not conceived, by his followers, the worshiper is absolved of any subjection to or dependence on his god. In neutral magic the user can bring into control the forces of nature for either good or bad, depending on his bent.

Much of what is popularly practiced as witchcraft today falls under the category of "neutral" magic or what is called "white magic." Dr. Kurt Koch in his book *Between Christ and Satan* defines white magic as that form of witchcraft which is allegedly promoted by the power of God for good. He gives an example of a case study to illustrate how white magic is used: "The owner of a certain farm hanged himself in his house. According to the popular belief of the villagers the man continued to haunt the place of his death. The relatives were advised to sweep out the whole house repeating the words, 'In the name of the Father, Son and Holy Ghost.' After this, the man's ghost would no longer trouble them. The relatives followed this unusual advice, but afterwards the farmer's wife was troubled by a strange feeling of unrest." Koch goes on to say that white magic utilizes "various Christian symbols . . . in conjunction with the number three. In some cases the names of the Trinity may be used, in others three Lord's prayers or three crosses or three Bible verses or even three candles may be used."⁶

Often black, neutral and white magic blend into each other in the practice of witchcraft. All three deny the devil, heaven and hell presented in the Bible but are convinced of the reality of the eternal life of the spirit or soul and the eternal circle of reincarnation whereby the just are rewarded and the unjust punished. (By whom, no one is quite sure!) There are also many common practices among the three camps, such as covens, spells, charms, incantations (or chants) and other rituals.

This chapter and the next will deal with the subject of witchcraft in general, both white and neutral magic. In chapter 9 we will consider Satanism, or black magic.

Two writings which shed light on the history of the witch cult are Charles Leland's *Aradia, or the Gospel of the Witches* (published in 1899) and *The Witch Cult in Western Europe,* containing the extensive research of Dr. Margaret Murray concerning the European witch trials of the same chronological period as *Aradia.*

Diana, the original witch

We have been referring to witchcraft as a religion. Why? In order to understand why witchcraft is indeed one of the earliest religions of man, let us look at its main tenets as described by T. C. Lethbridge. "The great deity who made the universe and ordered the lives of men was female. She was Diana who, to the Greek world, was known as Artemis. Diana was at first invisible, but she created light in the form of a male consort, Lucifer. He was represented by the sun, the greatest light known to men. Diana, queen of heaven and darkness, was represented by the greatest object in the night sky, the moon. A child of the union between light and darkness, Diana and Lucifer, was Magic and was known as Aradia. Aradia was sent to earth to teach this art to mankind. That is, she was, in the opinion of her devotees, a personage, known in the Hindu religion as an avatar, who taught them how to harness magic power."[7]

Aradia or Herodias is thought to have been as real a person as Krishna, Buddha or Christ.

According to legend, when Aradia had finished her instruction on earth, she told her pupils that she must leave them and return to heaven. If they wished any further instruction in the craft, they were to ask Diana, their Mother Goddess, "Queen of Witches All," for the necessary information. (Notice the strong parallel Aradia and Diana have to Christ and the Holy Spirit.)

Legend has it that Aradia's instruction included the meeting of her followers once a month, when the moon was full, in a secluded spot or a wood to adore Diana. At this time, they were to be naked (as a sign of freedom) and extinguish all the lights in order to play the game of "benevento" (apparently the same game played until recently by some Eskimos, who would put out their blubber lamps, grab the nearest woman and mate with her). After this, they held their sacred supper followed by drunken dancing and lovemaking.

Dr. Margaret Murray connects the earliest practice of the religion of witchcraft with the even older worship of Janus, the two-headed deity of the crossroads. "As Janus Quadritrons he presided over crossroads. It must be surely more than a coincidence that the Italian two-faced god of fertility should be the patron of crossroads, and that the

113

two-faced god of the witches should preside over fertility rites which were celebrated at crossroads."[8]

(I might make note at this point that the very same deity, called Carefour, is also worshiped by the Haitian mystery cult, Voodoo.)

The Mother Goddess, Diana, representing the force of fertility and creation, is symbolized today in witchcraft ceremonies by the wearing of silver or amber (never gold) jewelry and accessories. The Horned God, the ancient deity of the hunt who is symbolic of procreation and masculinity, is symbolized by horned skullcaps and similar regalia.[9]

Witchcraft, then, is a religion because it worships a deity or deities apart from and superior to man. It received its present name from the Celtic word *wicca*, meaning "craft of the wise." Witchcraft was very active up until the rise of Christianity (circa A.D. 30-35). Many ceremonies involved actual animal sacrifice—now replaced by symbolic gestures. It was not until the advent of Jesus Christ that witchcraft temporarily subsided. (The view of Christ and the Bible toward this pagan religion will be considered more fully in the next chapter.)

The positive message of eternal life through faith in Jesus Christ as the Son of God was enough to suppress the cult of witchcraft for the first few hundred years after Christ's death and resurrection. As the church became more and more concerned with ceremony, ritual and self-preservation, however, and less and less concerned with personal salvation by grace through faith alone, witchcraft again emerged with its man-made "salvation." By the thirteenth century, the "Christian" world was experiencing a real and visible conflict between religious tradition and pagan superstition. In what was later to follow, the simple biblical message of God's love as recorded by the apostle John was all but forgotten, "For God so loved the world, that He gave His only begotten Son, that whoever believes in Him should not perish but have eternal life."[10]

Persecution of witches

When Pope Innocent VIII not so innocently opened the proverbial Pandora's Box with the Bull of 1485, condemning to death any "known" witches, the religion of witchcraft and its followers began to suffer wholesale slaughter. Undoubtedly more non-followers than followers were put to death for crimes against church and state. "It was sufficient to be denounced as a follower of the Old Religion of witchcraft to be imprisoned,"[11] states Hanz Holzer, noted parapsychologist. "To be accused of this 'crime' made it mandatory to be tortured on the grounds that only under duress would a true heretic give out information about his 'sins.' Naturally, under torture, the victims would gladly confess to anything that would get them off the rack. At first, they simply told the truth about the Old Religion, but it did not fit in with what the persecutors wanted to hear.

"What was needed was a strong, imaginary story that would include a compact with the devil and consequently an admission of treason toward church and state. If the poor wretches did not understand what they were to say, the obliging torturers provided them with the necessary details, often preparing confessions that had only to be signed. This did not get the victims off, by any means. It merely cleared the decks for the next batch, while the signers were speedily dispatched via the stake or hanging, depending on local custom."[12]

While many died innocent of any crimes of involvement in witchcraft, the fact remains that during this time there were many true believers in the cult.

Sprenger (a name meaning "blaster"), one of the Grand Inquisitors of this period of torture and slaughter, was the first to enumerate in a book, *The Witches Hammer*, every sign and telltale mark of a witch. So thorough was his treatment of the subject, in fact, that no one—guilty or innocent—could escape his condemnation. Matthew Hopkins nearly 200 years later served as Witchfinder General of England with the same methodical judgment and authority.

During this era "whole communities of little children in Germany, Switzerland and Scotland were goaded on to false confession," relates Mrs. George C. Needham. "They were buried to the neck in pits, they were anchored in winter-cold waters, they were thrust into torturing machines, they were stuck with pins, they were dragged behind horses, they were made to swallow quantities of pins and vomit them up, their fingernails were drawn out with pincers and pins inserted in their places, they were stripped naked and dishonored to make them reveal the 'witch mark' upon their bodies. After such tortures, if they did not die under them, they were hanged or burned."[13]

Little change of attitude was seen in the Salem witch trials in the eighteenth century. The slightest manifestation of unusual behavior (absence from church services, an interest in music or dancing, let alone true psychic ability and powers) was often sufficient cause for a citizen to be jailed and tried as a witch. (Even a mole on a woman indicated the presence of a third nipple and was used to brand her as a witch.) The methods of trial were often cruel and unfair—mere mockeries of justice. Often, if an alleged witch survived prolonged "dunkings," she (or he) was tried by fallacious standards and condemned to burn at the stake.

History leaves no doubt in one's mind that these atrocities committed in the name of the Christian religion have no relation to true biblical Christianity and the teachings of Christ Himself.

We must be careful in our treatment of the historical persecution of witches, however, not to make two mistakes: First, to demean the reality of demons and evil spirits, and second, to assume that because human persecution of witches was sadistic and often unjust God does not Himself condemn true witchcraft and those who practice it. Though many people were unjustly condemned and killed, still there were those who were actually possessed by evil spirits. Demon possession is neither new nor mere fantasy nor superstition.[14] God calls the practice of witchcraft "detestable to the Lord" and, demanding the death penalty, "You shall not allow a sorceress to live."[15]

117

From 1736 (when witchcraft was removed from the list of capital offenses in the American colonies) until the present, there has been little persecution of superstitious beliefs in America. Quite the contrary is the case in Mexico, however, where in 1968 a witch was hung by sixteen townspeople for having killed a little girl by sorcery. Or in Hungary, where just recently three men and three women were tried for attempting to burn at the stake an elderly woman whom they believed "put the evil eye" on one of their young relatives.

The interest of the general public in witchcraft today can be traced back to the Englishman Gerald Gardner, who in 1954 published a book called *Witchcraft Today*. Gardner had been received into a coven and was one of the first witches to divulge the coven's practices in writing. His second book, *The Meaning of Witchcraft*, published in 1959, told further of the pre-Christian history of the religion of "Wicca."

Gardner's cult received excessive publicity for their all-nude rituals. By 1964, the year of his death, there were "Gardnerites" throughout all of Great Britain. Numerous splits in the Gardner cult since its founder's death account for much of the wide divergence in belief and practice today. At least half-a-dozen groups are still heavily saturated with sexually perverted rites, while many have migrated to the opposite pole in their puritanical methodology. Still, most believers will trace their cult ancestry back to the worship of Diana or her ethnic counterparts.

Even though witchcraft is now popularly practiced and accepted in most societies, there are places where the fear of being unjustly accused of being thought to be a witch still lives. The Dutch village of Ouddwater, for instance, maintains to this day as a curiosity a weighing station that awards certificates to visitors.[16] These certificates prove that the bearer should not be burned at the stake as a witch. Because witches were said to have no souls (a claim made by non-witches), they were presumed to weigh less than normal people of the same size. This Dutch weighing station proves that the individual weighs what he should and is therefore human, not supernatural.

The witchcraft cult is still very much alive. Many are sincerely seeking answers to their spiritual quests through this pagan religion of Diana worship.

While it is true that God's in His heaven, all is *not* right with the world. The ancient myth that a man's soul actually weighs something is childishly humorous when compared to the present myth that a man's soul can be at peace without the presence and power of almighty God.

Footnotes for Chapter 7

1. Arturo F. Gonzalez, Jr., "The Witchcraft Revival," *The Christian Herald*, June 1970, p. 25.

2. Gonzalez, "The Witchcraft Revival," p. 25.

3. Gonzalez, "The Witchcraft Revival," p. 27.

4. Gonzalez, "The Witchcraft Revival," pp. 25, 26.

5. Gonzalez, "The Witchcraft Revival," p. 25.

6. Kurt Koch, D.D., *Between Christ and Satan* (Berghausan BD. Germany, Evangelization Publishers, 1961), pp. 92, 93. U.S. edition: Grand Rapids: Kregel Publications, 1968.

7. T.C. Lethbridge, *Witches* (New York: The Citadel Press, 1968), pp. 13,14.

8. Hanz Holzer, *The Truth About Witchcraft* (Garden City, N.Y.: Doubleday, 1969), p. 54.

9. Holzer, *The Truth About Witchcraft*, pp. 12, 13.

10. John 3:16.

11. Holzer, *The Truth About Witchcraft*, p. 64.

12. Holzer, *The Truth About Witchcraft*, pp. 64, 65.

13. Mrs. George C. Needham, *Angels and Demons* (Chicago: Moody Press), p. 76.

14. For an in-depth study of demons—their reality and activity—read *Demons in the World Today* by Dr. Merrill F. Unger (Wheaton: Tyndale House, 1971).

15. Deuteronomy 18:12 and Exodus 22:18.

16. Gonzalez, "The Witchcraft Revival," p. 27.

"Witchcraft is so enduring that it admits of no remedy by human operation."

St. Thomas Aquinas
Sententiae

CHAPTER 8

The Ghost of Witches Present

How many times have you met someone who is left-handed, attended a country fair, danced around a Maypole, wished someone who sneezed "God bless you" or watched a child ride a hobbyhorse?

Did you know that these, plus many more, have a special significance in the old religion of witchcraft?

The *left hand* was considered devilish since "left" meant "evil" or "sinister." (Even today in many Eastern nations you must not give something to someone with your left hand!) Spilled salt—an unlucky omen—is to be thrown over the left shoulder into the face of the devil himself. The *Maypole dance,* which is innocently practiced by many youngsters today, has its roots in the early religion's unabashed worship of sex. Such worship took the form of dances around a totem-type image, with explicit charms and amulets worn around the neck.

Wishing someone who sneezes a simple, *God bless you* is said to have originally been a prayer that the devil would not fly up his nose when he sneezed since his soul simultaneously came out his nostrils. The *country fair* was first begun as an "esbath" or regular meeting of the witch cult in fields and forests where all sorts of revelry would take place.

Hobbyhorses find their origin in the custom which required female witches to bring their broom with them to the meetings and enter the "sacred precincts" of the circle astride their "staff of office." Thus they appeared to be riding their brooms as horses.

Broomsticks are thought by some authorities to be another sexual symbol while attributed by others to the witches' concept of domestic order and cleanliness. The wearing of *birthstones* is of pagan background also, as different stones were said to possess different powers.

And *Hallowee*n or *All Hallows Eve* (October 31) is still one of the four major holidays (or "sabbaths" as they are called) for witches as it celebrates the coming of the fall season. Others are "Candlemas" or Brigid's Day (February 2—introducing winter), "May Eve" (April 30—introducing spring) and "Lamas" (July 31—introducing summer).

Perhaps it's not so strange, when one thinks about

the continuing popularity of witchcraft down through the ages, that the celebration of Halloween in "Christian" America is as popular, if not more so, as the holy day of Easter celebrating the resurrection of the Lord Jesus Christ. (Also interesting is the fact that while the Christian celebrations of Christmas and Easter have their secular counterparts in Santa and the Easter Bunny, the debased nature of Halloween remains intact!)

As we study the religion of Witchcraft, we must be careful in considering the subject to evaluate it as it is practiced today—not just by its past history and superstition but by its present beliefs. Sybil Leek, the widely-renowned witch, astrologer, writer and lecturer, claims that "witchcraft is a return to a nature religion. It teaches people their place in the universe and helps them see religion much more clearly—as the real thing and not as a fantasy world."[1] While it is true that much of witchcraft remains the same in theory, doctrine and practice, it is equally as true that much has been changed to accommodate itself to a changed society.

There is much myth still in existence when it comes to the subject. It ranges from an inability to believe in any kind of spiritual world or spiritual beings at all to one philosophy summed up by Professor Peter H. Rossi, Chairman of the Department of Social Relations at Johns Hopkins University, who says: "I am not sure that I believe in good spirits but I have the uncanny feeling that there might be evil spirits."[2] There are others who believe that all witches are good, decent, law-abiding folk like Samantha on the TV show "Bewitched."

Witchcraft is relegated to a harmless pastime for those who are inclined in that direction.

In an age of supposed enlightenment such as ours, it is amazing to discover how very little most people actually know about the religion of Witchcraft and its tenets and practices. Blindly closing their eyes to the entire witchcraft scene, they prefer to believe that the involvement of so many people in witchcraft is nothing more than a bad dream which will soon end.

Witchcraft ceremony

"Know your enemy" is perhaps a practical motto to keep in mind regarding witchcraft. We can best feel the impact of the cult's doctrines by observing a more or less typical present-day "esbath" or weekly meeting. (Please—we are not recommending actual attendance at such a meeting. There are many stable sources of information short of doing this— the following description is hoped to be one of them.)

The coven (never more than thirteen people), meaning "brotherhood" or "congregation," meets in secret with curtains drawn and blinds pulled. In attendance are usually middle and upper middle class "followers," some with their mates, others preferring to come alone, and all with special names known only to the other members of the coven.[3] After each has bathed in salt water (for purification purposes), they assemble around a nine-foot circle outlined on the floor with chalk or white rope.

Visible only by the light of two candles, the

members are often naked—the nudity we are told is to allow a free flow of body energy from each of the members to the rest of the group.

On the crudely constructed altar rest a silver chalice, a hazelwood wand (another sexual symbol) as well as a small caldron (representing the Mother Goddess, Diana). Accompanying these are a brass censer of burning incense, a pentacle (a five-pointed metal star engraved with witch signs) which represents the earth, a scourge (or small whip), a bowl of salt (symbolizing purification), a black-handled "athame" (or sword) representing air and a length of cord (symbolizing the spirit that unites all elements).

In addition to various "exercises," the group may at times sing or listen to a flutist prior to the reading from *The Book of the Shadows* or a similar volume. Unavailable to most people and usually altered to fit each coven, *The Book of the Shadows* speaks in detail of Witchcraft dogma and ritual. Another popular book among witches is the *6th and 7th Book of Moses*, which is particularly widespread in European witchcraft covens. The oldest editions date back to the sixteenth century. Dr. Kurt Koch, in discussing this particular work, says of it: "The tragedy is that this book is still being printed today." He goes on to say: "The appearance of the name Moses in the original title is only a deception. Moses himself had nothing to do with magic. Magicians, however, have tried to elevate him to the position of their patron saint, using as an argument in support of this the fact that he was victorious over the Egyptian magicians in Exodus 7:8,9. But this is

127

a devilish misunderstanding of the prophetic endowment of this Old Testament man of God."[4]

After the reading from *The Book of the Shadows* there is the ceremonial scourging or cleansing followed by an opportunity for those who feel led to share a personal request with the rest of the group. Each request is then chanted by the entire coven in a vigorous and optimistic anticipation of the result. This usually concludes the meeting, after which the members dress and fellowship together in another part of the house.

Often the witchcraft ceremony involves the use of psychedelic drugs or salves such as belladonna, aconite or the amanita mushroom, which is either eaten raw or brewed. The "high" produced from psychedelics can make one feel like he is actually "flying" (the most probable explanation for the experiences of witches who claim to have flown through the air). The word translated "sorcery" in the New Testament (i.e., Galatians 5:20) is, in the original Greek text, the word *pharmakeia* and has reference primarily to psychedelic drugs used in exercising the magical arts.[5]

"The salve evidently produces pretty much the same reactions in most people,"[6] Hanz Holzer reports. Several years ago a German researcher, Dr. Erich Will Peuckert, faithfully followed the prescription for a sixteenth-century witches' ointment and concocted the same salve, with which he then anointed himself and an attorney friend. After the two men came out of a trancelike condition twenty hours later, their experiences matched almost exactly. Both had "flown through the air" to a witches' sabbath, "seen the devil" and partaken in similar sexual debauchery and practices—all in their minds, of course. Thus they had, in 1960, followed the path of fantasy experienced by the witches of earlier times.[7]

I might add that these supposed visions of both God and Satan are not limited only to those involved in witchcraft. Similar experiences are very common today among those who have used or are using hallucinogenic drugs such as LSD. Drug abuse and the occult are often knit closely together—a strong evidence of Satanic influence in the "mind-expanding" drugs.

The basic elements of witchcraft theology are first, that man is born innocent and not guilty, and second, that spiritual life after death is accomplished in every person by reincarnation. It is also believed that one must go through three "stages," each year in duration, before he or she can obtain full powers as a witch.

An important thing to realize about witches is that they are not all early African Voodoo worshipers who torment, maim or kill their victims with fear as is commonly depicted in many "B" movies. The psychic power of a witch coven is most closely related to a form of group telepathy. The result of the combined thought waves of the group, the "cone of power" as it is called, is a neutral force which can be directed only by the head witch. Whereas most of the thought power has to do with healing, both physical and emotional, sometimes the "cone" is directed against a person or group of people.

Scriptural viewpoint

Interviews with various witches bear out the theory that many have come out of churches which do not preach the Bible and Christianity as a living faith, but merely as a moral or ethical code. "I never met a former Unitarian or other 'liberal' Christian who sought out witchcraft," says parapsychologist Holzer, "simply because the liberal Christian churches are close enough to the ideals of the craft not to warrant leaving it for a coven."[8] In both the liberal churches to which Mr. Holzer refers and witchcraft, Jesus Christ is viewed not as the actual Son of God but as only a symbol of deity, an empty "God-word," full of empathy but void of content.

At the heart of witchcraft is a rejection of God and an exaltation of man to godlike stature. It is chiefly for this reason that witch Madge Worthington boldly predicts that "Eventually it (witchcraft) will supersede Christianity—certainly by the end of the century, if not before. Paganism is a natural and beautiful religion and Christianity is a frustrated one."[9]

In the light of biblical Christianity, witchcraft is an idolatrous and misleading practice. The Bible teaches that salvation is a gift from God, completely and entirely offered from God to man, not vice versa, without the help of man himself. "He saved us, not on the basis of deeds which we have done in righteousness,"[10] Paul says, "For by grace you have been saved through faith; and that not of yourselves, it is the gift of God; not as a result of works, that no one should boast."[11] The concept of man perfecting himself through reincarnation or any other physical, emotional, mental or spiritual means is completely contrary to the teachings of Scripture.

Cognizance of true human nature, if viewed objectively, would alone invalidate the idea of "innocence" to which witches subscribe. To say that one is born innocent is invariably to place the blame for evil on the society into which the child is raised or at least on some "outside influence." How, one might ask, would society become an evil influence if, from its inception, each member was innocent? Such a stand clearly violates the teaching of Scripture that "all have sinned and fall short of the glory of God"[12] and that it was "while we were yet sinners, Christ died for us."[13] "Behold, I was brought forth in iniquity," David cries out in the Psalms, "and in sin my mother conceived me."[14]

The teaching of reincarnation is opposed to the biblical truth that for the believer in Jesus Christ to be absent from the body is to be present with the Lord.[15] Jesus' parable of the rich man and Lazarus[16] teaches that after death there is no "second chance" for those who have lived a life apart from God and Christ. The concept too that one must go through stages of reincarnation denies the simplicity of faith in the living God through belief in His Son.

The gospel of Christ, as opposed to the gospel of the witches, is not limited to those with superior intelligence or to those who would attempt to reach perfection through self-denial or bodily discipline. It is, in fact, oftentimes more difficult for these "self-righteous" people to come to repentance than for others who realize their need.

And finally, Christianity opposes witchcraft's concept of the many ways through which God can be known. The experience of the student who was able to "make an end run around the Holy Spirit to God Himself" is a frequent occurrence with the use of drugs like LSD. I have spoken with many students who will testify to actually having "seen God" on such occasions. The "god" that the drugged individual sees, however, is not the real God but a false representation—the concoction of an evil spirit. The mind under the control of hallucinogenic drugs is a playground for Satanic activity.

It is the Christian's belief that God is knowable only through His Son. Jesus said, "He who has seen Me has seen the Father"[17] and "I and the Father are one."[18] It is the Holy Spirit of God, not a psychedelic drug trip, who reveals God to man.

Therefore, the fact that the Bible speaks against drug abuse and the fact that God is knowable only through faith, not through drugs or any other means, would lead us to the necessary conclusion that the "god" which is seen through drugs and witchcraft practices is not the God of the Bible but rather the god of this world—Satan.

Here, again, are the areas in which Christianity and witchcraft come into direct conflict doctrinally.

First, the philosophy that man can earn his "salvation" by working harder and denying himself so that he will be reincarnated into a more perfect specimen is completely contradictory to the teachings of the New Testament.

Secondly, witchcraft's concept of man being born innocent and becoming corrupted is contrary to the

Bible, which says that man is born a sinner and unable to atone for that sin apart from Jesus Christ's shed blood as a final sacrifice for sin.

Thirdly, there is no concept of reincarnation to be found in either the Old or New Testaments. The Bible teaches that each man dies once and then is judged before the throne of a perfect, righteous God.[19]

Fourthly, the Bible presents a clearcut method for knowing the unseeable, untouchable God—through simple faith in Jesus Christ and His claims to be God in the flesh who took man's death on Himself and paid the price for the penalty of our sin. All that witchcraft presents as a possible road to God—whether it be drugs, chanting, self-denial, positive thinking or any such man-made thing—is fallacious and impotent.

The conflict between witchcraft and Christianity is no more clearly seen in the Bible than in the 19th chapter of the book of Acts.[20] Paul had been preaching the gospel of Jesus Christ in the city of Ephesus, a city which was heavily immersed in the occult practices of the time. Many of these occultists came to believe in Jesus Christ under Paul's preaching. We are told that as they believed they "kept coming, confessing and disclosing their practices." "And many of those who practiced magic brought their books together and began burning them in the sight of all; and they counted up the price of them and found it fifty thousand pieces of silver." (This amount is roughly equivalent to $10,000 today.) Under the convicting power of the Holy Spirit, these men, many of whom were actively involved in the practices of witchcraft, came to see the truth of Jesus Christ. Their sorcery books were no longer needed. Their charts, amulets and icons were suddenly powerless. These had been replaced by a living, vital, dynamic God who could give them the true meaning for life that sorcery and witchcraft fell short of providing.

The Scriptures record that due to the power of the Word of God, witchcraft was given up for the only True Faith. Man had challenged God with his puny efforts to perfect himself and to control the world around him, and had soon accepted his own defeat as inevitable.

"So the word of the Lord was growing mightily and prevailing."

It is interesting, isn't it, to see where ultimate supernatural power really lies.

Footnotes for Chapter 8

1. Arturo F. Gonzalez, Jr., "The Witchcraft Revival," *The Christian Herald,* June, 1970, p. 27.

2. Gonzalez, "The Witchcraft Revival," p. 27.

3. Witches today are in no way similar to their fairy-tale counterparts. John Kerr, *The Mystery and Magic of the Occult* (Philadelphia: Fortress Press, 1971), p. 79, says on this particular point: "Our image of witches comes to us from the three hags in *Macbeth,* stirring their filthy cauldrons and muttering weird chants; from Grimm's *Fairy Tales,* where the long crooked fingers point their warts at you while the witch cackles; and from the late Walt Disney who filled our eyes with such monstrous females in his cartoon films."

4. The psychological and spiritual harm in the very possession of such magical books as these is illustrated by Kurt Koch, D.D., *Between Christ and Satan* (Berghausan BD. Germany, Evangelization Publishers, 1961,) pp.167-182. U.S. edition: Grand Rapids: Kregel Publications, 1968.

5. T. Witton Davies, "Witchcraft," *International Standard Bible Encyclopedia,* Ed. by James Orr (Grand Rapids: Eerdmans, 1939), vol. 3, p. 1964.

6. Hanz Holzer, *The Truth About Witchcraft* (Garden City, N.Y.: Doubleday, 1969), p. 73.

7. Holzer, *The Truth About Witchcraft,* p. 73.

8. Holzer, *The Truth About Witchcraft,* p. 34.

9. Gonzalez, "The Witchcraft Revival," p. 26.

10. Titus 3:5.

11. Ephesians 2:8,9.

12. Romans 3:23.

13. Romans 5:8.

14. Psalm 51:5.

15. Colossians 2:5.

16. Luke 16:19-31.

17. John 14.9.

18. John 10:30.

19. Hebrews 9:27.

20. Acts 19:17-20.

*"Better to reign in hell
than serve in heaven."*

Milton
Paradise Lost

CHAPTER 9

The Devil Made Me Do It

Perhaps no one is so misunderstood as the Satanist.

To some, he is the devil himself, motivated by a diabolical ambition to be God. Sacrificing infants on altars of blood while conjuring up a death potion in the back room, the Satanist is the epitome of all that is base and degenerate. To others, the self-proclaimed Satanist is a good-natured jokester who lives in a world of fantasy and is as harmless as the proverbial absentminded professor. This type of evildoer finds his ecstasy in dressing up in black regalia and wearing his hexogram necklace and skull bracelet while being photographed eating devil's food cake.

To say the least, the Satanist presents a mysterious and many-sided picture to the uninitiated spectator. Still and all, most people today, like their grandparents, have a strange fear of this phenomenon and an even stronger feeling of helplessness regarding what to do about it. All around us we seem to see a world gone mad in its pursuit of Satanic activities. People everywhere have an uncanny interest in the works of the devil.

Just who is this person called Satan? Is he real . . . or merely a myth? Might he really have power over men's minds and souls? Is Satan worship something that can harm the human psyche? Or is it merely another one of many fascinations to which man attaches himself for a season—until something new comes along?

I believe that we can clear up some misconceptions about the devil by focusing our attention toward three separate areas. For clarity's sake, I will break them down into (1) the Satan faddist, (2) the Satan cultist, and (3) the real Satan.

The Satan faddist

It wasn't surprising to me when three of the students raised their hands in reply to my question, "How many of you have ever been into Satanism?" After all, I had received as much, if not more response, from hundreds of students in schools and churches throughout California. What was surprising, though, was the circumstance surrounding this particular session. Ten years ago, such a thing would never have occurred. But there I was, upon invitation by the teacher and several students, lecturing in a high school Contemporary American Problems class on the subject of Satanism and Black Magic!

I tried to recall studying such an intriguing subject several years ago in my senior C.A.P. class, but the only contemporary problems I could remember were Castro's takeover of Cuba, Hawaii's admission as the 50th state and Khrushchev's threat to bury me.

The subject of black magic, with its infamous history of blood sacrifice, ritual killings and the like has become a very "in" thing—especially with students. Conversation on campus about who is the best student witch or about some new book on black magic is commonplace. Witchcraft and magic shops can be found today in almost every large American city, a very recent phenomenon.

I seriously question whether some of what we see calling itself Satanism is a real cult or another fad.

Certainly the owner of the Hermetics Workshop in Los Angeles would be quick to defend the sincerity of her customers. But a glance around the shelves at the sequined skulls, plastic crucifixes, Jewish stars and homemade sex potions reveals that crass commercialism has taken its toll with the most dedicated of witches. In fact, at least a dozen shops in the Los Angeles area specialize in dispensing all the tools necessary to the practice of magic and/or Satanism; from a $3 amulet of the Egyptian symbol of life (as found in *The Book of the Dead*, incidentally) to Satanic crosses, tannis root, graveyard clay and black cat hair.

Nationwide clientele (composed of college professors, actors and businessmen) frequent occult shops, buy off-beat newspapers and scan public libraries in search of the latest avant-garde happenings in the realm of the supernatural. To most of these Satanism is merely a passing fancy which provides them with innumerable intriguing conversations at a cocktail party. As soon as something even more intriguing comes along, they will drop Satanism and move into whatever might be the next new "thing."

There are those, of course, who take it a little more seriously but refuse to be labeled "religious fanatics" or to have anything to do with actual demonic activities. A particular group is the Church of Satan, with home offices in San Francisco, which boasts a national membership of over 10,000 active parishioners. Its High Priest or "Black Pope" is one Anton La Vey, D.S.T. ("Doctor of Satanic Theology").

The Church of Satan came into existence in 1966 when La Vey was inspired to shave his head, put on a Roman collar and announce the new "Satanic Age." The church's first major publicity was given to La Vey's Satanic wedding (performed in front of a nude woman reclining upon a makeshift altar), celebrated with the chants, decorum and macabre usually associated with many second-rate horror movies. Soon after this, the christening of infants became a regular observance, and a "Satanic funeral service" was held by La Vey for one of the members, Mr. Ed Olsen, a Navy man, who had been killed in an automobile crash. It was Olsen's widow who concluded that he would have wanted to be buried with "full Satanic honors."

Basing his operations from a three-story, thirteen-room Victorian home in a San Francisco residential district, La Vey surrounds himself with the traditional open coffins, tombstones, skeletons and black cats so necessary to his trade. Absorbed in interviews, rituals and conversations clarifying his views as expressed in his "Satanic Bible," he finds little time to shepherd his ever-growing flock. Many applicants sincerely interested in doing evil are rejected by La Vey in favor of the "beautiful people," (some of them well-monied) who desire more of a social club/therapy group than a contract with the devil. "(Many) feel that this is a clearinghouse for perverts, sex creeps, real losers, people that have been rejected by society. And it isn't," says La Vey. "Because the true image of the Satanist, from the beginning of what, by one name or another would be considered Satanism, is that of the Master, the Leader, the controller of societies, the image makers. All these people that have been winners have practiced intrinsically a Satanic concept of life."[1]

The Church of Satan seems more concerned with letting people do what they want, regardless of society's laws and mores, than with forcing them to worship a personal supreme deity. By his own admission, La Vey expresses that "my church is based on (self) indulgence. Eventually, I want to build pleasure domes—retreats for my followers. I think a church should be something people can't wait to get into instead of a place they can't wait to get out

141

of."[2] La Vey and his followers subscribe to a philosophy of total freedom, sexual as well as personal. "We believe in the pleasures of the flesh, living to the hilt, enjoying all there is to be on earth," La Vey admits.[3]

There are those followers of the Church of Satan who are dead serious in their pursuit of Satan, but these might very well be in the minority. (This type of person will be discussed in the next section on the "Satan cultist.")

In the main, popular Satanism is often merely a game, a kind of relief from a pressured environment. At best, the Satan fad is a sick expression of man's natural selfishness and greed, which shows itself in a full-scale pursuit of hedonism. When asked, "Have you seen the Devil?" La Vey coyly replied, "Oh yes, every time I shave!"[4] Take care of yourself first, give yourself all pleasure first and let everyone else do the same. If the "real world" disappoints you and doesn't live up to what you want it to be, if things don't go your way as often as you would like them to, then Satanism offers a solution and an easy way out.

It is this need to escape from reality to which most of men's philosophies and religious systems address themselves, but it is this author's deep conviction that regardless of how "odd" or even how "traditional" that form of escape may be, it is doomed to failure when it is not a faith based upon the timeless truths of the Word of God.

The Satan faddist does not adhere to the teachings of the Bible but in fact directly opposes them. The essence of sin, as the Bible describes it, is the desire for self-satisfaction—man exalted to the place of God. This is the Satanist doctrine. Therefore, even though his "fad" may seem quite harmless, he is nevertheless opposed to the will of God. Being "just a little bit" of a Satanist is like being "just a little bit" pregnant. You can't play at devil worship and hope to avoid its long-range consequences. The fad may pass, but Satan-worship in any form will leave spiritual scars.

Secondly, one who is attracted to the worship of Satan is capable of being led further and further into the occult. What might have started out as a fad may turn into a mania—a mania that can result in spiritual separation from God for eternity.

So next time you're thinking about a hobby, might I suggest macrame or finger-painting? The Satan faddist almost always gets more than he bargained for.

The Satan cultist

As is true with any fad, there are those involved in the Satan craze who sincerely believe. These are the ones who shun the commercial wrappings of their religion, those who rebel against the gimmicks and publicity connected with their craft. To them Satanism is more than a passing fancy. It is a way of life, a style of behavior and a process of thought that is far different from yours or mine.

One such follower was Patrick Michael Newell of Vineland, New Jersey. Many of Mike's high school classmates had known him to be a bit strange because of all of his magical studies, Satanic ritual

143

and occasional animal sacrifices. But they had never given all this much thought—it was just "his own thing." Not until that gruesome day in mid-July, 1971, did the people who knew Mike come to realize just how deep his Satanic philosophy had affected his life.[5]

Mike, as reported by his lawyer, had convinced two of his close friends, Richard Williams (18) and Wayne Sweikert (17), to accompany him to a deserted pond in the foothills of southern New Jersey. After conducting a brief service to the devil, Mike instructed the two boys to bind his hands and feet with adhesive tape and, because they were his "friends," to push him into the pond. Williams and Sweikert did as instructed and watched him sink— not to be seen again until his body was found three days later.

What drove this 20-year-old youth to such a diabolical, untimely and unnecessary death?

It seems that Newell's studies in black magic had led him to the conclusion that any loyal Satan-worshiper who is murdered by his friends would be "reborn" as a captain of over forty legions of Satan's demons. The scene at Clear Pond was Mike's attempt to be recast into that role.

"But it's not that common," you might say. "That was a one-in-a-million case."

What about the California schoolteacher in Orange County whose heart, lungs and liver were found missing from her grave and were later found to have been used by her murderers as part of a sacrifice to the devil?

Twenty-year-old Steve Hurd, as his attorney says,

144

took part in the brutal slaying of Mrs. Florence Brown along with two other youths because their religion had taught them that it was all right to "snuff people out" as long as a portion of the victim's body was sacrificed to Satan.[6]

Interestingly enough, all three members of this "Devil Cult" were on their way to San Francisco to see "a man who considers himself akin to Satan, head of the devil cultists."

"Hurd claims he really believes in the devil," his attorney later testified.[7] This fact was well illustrated when authorities observed that Hurd's main fear after his arrest by Orange County police was not so much the upcoming trial but rather the presence of a Holy Bible in his cell.

In July of 1971, 22-year-old Kim Brown, a long-haired Satanist who swears she once "saw the devil" was convicted of manslaughter for stabbing a 62-year-old man to death. "I really enjoyed killing him," she said, between her private worship services to Satan in a Miami jail.[8] There seems to be no doubt in Miss Brown's mind as to whom she worships.

As sick as these events are, they are not the only evidence of Satan worship in the United States. "Tales of witchcraft cults that sacrifice animals and turn humans into 'slaves of Satan' are coming out of the mountains that form a bucolic backdrop to the Northern California coastal town of Santa Cruz," reports the *Los Angeles Herald Examiner*.[9] The wholesale slaughter of animals in the area is alarming to the director of the Santa Cruz animal shelter, who comments that "the skin is cut away without even marking the flesh. The really strange thing is that each of these dogs has been drained of blood." The conclusion of most authorities is that there is at least one group of Satanists somewhere in Northern California that worships with blood sacrifices.

Similar conclusions have been reached in San Jose, where two young girls were found stabbed more than 300 times with "virtually no trace of blood where the victims' bodies were found," claims Mr. Barton Collins, Chief of Detectives.[10]

Case after case of similar Satanic worship in every part of the United States involving obscene and grotesque ceremonies could be mentioned at this time, but we need not pursue the subject any further to establish our premise. The truth is that there is an alarmingly phenomenal increase in devil worship in the United States, most of which has come within the last five years!

We do not dare write off this obsession with Satan as mere fad or fairy tale. On the contrary, the current obsession with Satan and blood sacrifice is a strong sign of the revival of black magic, a craft which has been with us for at least 3,000 years. The Old Testament relates time after time occasions where black magic was used by those opposing the nation of Israel.

The Egyptian occultist, Rollo Ahmed, analyzes the Satanist cults of history in his *Complete Book of Witchcraft* and notes that "Many people famous in history are mentioned as having had dealings with witchcraft." Scanning historical records, Rollo Ahmed names Sextus (the son of Pompey), Benvenuto Cellini, Catherine de Medici and the Count

146

de Cagliostro as just a few. Gilles de Raiz and his sorcerer, Francis Prelati, were executed in 1440 for the mutilation, torture, rape and the murder of many persons, including little children. In 1610, Hungarian countess and Satanist Elizabeth Bathony was tried and executed after the dead bodies of some 50 girls were found chained in the cellar of her castle.[11]

Black masses, hardly a new thing, have been performed for the past 500 years, perhaps the most horrible series being that of Catherine de Shayes (La Voisine) in 1670, after which investigators found her furnace piled with the charred bodies of scores of children.

The black mass as it is celebrated today is essentially the same as it was several hundred years ago, with the possible exception of less animal and human sacrifices. Though there have been rumors of occasional infant sacrifices during some black masses of the '70s, the probability of this being a common practice is rare (and its documentation ever more rare).[12] In most cases the Catholic mass is mimicked with all its rites being turned against Christ and the Church. (For example, the black crucifix hung upside down over the black altar with black candles, hymns sung backwards and the name of the Lord Jesus Christ omitted, spit upon or in some other way desecrated by celebrants.) Often such masses are performed by a defrocked priest or someone impersonating a priest. Much use is made of ancient "secret" books, chants and incantations, while an aura of sexual perversity and obscenity pervades the ceremonies. A noticeable distinction

147

between the black masses of old and those of today is the absence of the stereotyped "bad guy" in favor of the more "respectable" members of society. Business and professional men and women form a large part of the constituency of such forbidden cults. (It should also be noted that in the majority of black magic practices, drugs—especially those of the hallucinogenic variety—play a vital role.)

Books such as Rollo Ahmed's and *The Black Arts* by Richard Cavendish, are but two of the more than two million volumes on Satanism and witchcraft available in libraries throughout the world.[13] The practice of black magic in all its perversity has left no small mark on the annals of recorded history.

The increasing pursuit of the occult in general and Satanism or black magic in particular should be a signpost of the direction in which society is moving. While it is true that still only a very small percentage of Americans are involved in these sadistic quests, it is nevertheless a commentary on our "enlightened" culture that man should be so inclined. When, according to estimates by Father Richard Woods of Chicago's Loyola University, there are some 80,000 disciples of witchcraft in the United States alone and with that number growing rapidly, we had better take a second look at the reasons behind its popularity.[14]

Why does a college professor, for example, leave a well-paying teaching position to become an initiate in a witch coven? Why should such a deity as Satan demand and receive the affection of hundreds of thousands of college and university students across the country? Why are those like Mike Newell willing to suffer and even die for what they believe?

I believe that first and foremost there is a definite, though often suppressed, need for a personal faith in something beyond oneself. Religion is, after all, man's attempt to reach God—to have a relationship with a supreme deity. And black magic is one of the oldest religions of man.

C. S. Lewis, in his book *The Problem of Pain,* tells us, "To be God—to be like God and to share His goodness in creaturely response—to be miserable—these are the only three alternatives."[15] Man will either be his own god or he will worship something he deems is god or he will be miserable. We have previously pointed out the truth that in all societies and in all periods of human history, man has felt a universal need to believe in a god or gods.

The Bible teaches that there is only one true God, the Father of the Lord Jesus Christ, who showed His love for man by sending His Son in the flesh to our earth. Lewis puts it well when he says that God has landed on this enemy-occupied world in human form. And the enemy who is currently occupying God's territory is none other than Satan himself, the "prince of darkness."

In order for a faith to be valid, it must not contradict itself. What puzzles me so greatly about those who claim to be Satan worshipers is the hypocrisy of a faith which preaches love yet manipulates hate, and even murder, to achieve its ends. Secondly, Satanism is in many ways a counterfeit of Christianity. Nearly every observance of the true Satanist is a faulty or perverted copy of some form of Christian

149

liturgy. The backward hymns, inverted crucifix and use of the number three are all antitheses of Christian observances.

Belief in a counterfeit god presupposes the existence of an original. The god of the Satanist is, at best, a faulty imitation of the true God—offering nothing but counterfeit dreams and shattered reality.

Now, at the risk of being thought a fanatic, let me share with you what I believe to be an even greater form of Satanism than that which we have just been discussing. Whereas black magic as it is called boasts a fairly small following, this form of Satanism lays claim to the lives of the majority of men and women in the world today.

The unfortunate thing is that most people do not know who Satan really is—and what he is capable of doing. They have been taught that he is either nonexistent and imaginary, therefore irrelevant, or else that he is all-powerful and therefore symbolic ultimate good.

Actually, neither of these extreme pictures portrays the real Satan—the Satan whose history and actions run throughout the Old and New Testaments.

The real Satan

Satan is usually thought of as a fad or else pictured as some fiendish, cloven-footed monster brandishing a pitchfork in one hand and hot coals in the other. What most people do not realize is that the stereotyped picture of the monkey-like devil with

150

large ears, horns and a tail is a product of the very recent past. Such a picture is largely the result of the work of a few highly-imaginative artists from the twelfth to the twentieth centuries. The Bible reveals nothing of such a visual monstrosity, as we will see.

"Satan is a living creature," McCandlish Phillips verifies in his book, *The Bible, the Supernatural, and the Jews*. "He is not corporeal. He is a spiritual being, but that does not make him any less real. The fact that he is invisible and powerful greatly serves him in the pursuit of his cause. The idea that Satan is a term for a generalized influence of evil—instead of the name of a specific living personality—is a strictly anti-biblical idea.

"The name Satan does not speak of an impersonal influence. It speaks of a single, identifiable, distinct living being with a will, a personality, and a highly directed intelligence."[16]

In order to understand more fully who Satan is, we must turn to the Bible as our source, for it alone is the book which most clearly and truthfully describes the person of Satan. (As you read this section, please realize that there are volumes that can be written about Satan and that this book by no means exhausts all the information available. It is a subject which must be dealt with carefully and should be taken seriously by every reader concerned with his spiritual well-being.)

If, as the Bible claims, there *is* a real Satan, then to be forewarned might possibly mean being forearmed.

First of all, the Bible teaches us that Satan at one

time was a created spirit, an "angel of light"[17] who dwelt close to God. By his own decision, Satan rebelled because of his pride and was cast out of God's presence along with the other spirit beings who had joined in the rebellion. He was once—and still is—a beautiful creation of God, contrary to the popular image of him as ugly and fiendish.[18]

Secondly, Satan is a master of subtlety. This trait was exhibited toward man from the very beginnings when Satan spoke to Eve and convinced her that she would not die if she broke God's commandment forbidding her to eat of the tree of the knowledge of good and evil.[19] Today Satan's subtlety takes the form of convincing men and women that there really is no devil. In so doing, he verifies his character. By creating disbelief in his own existence, he acts true to form, fulfilling his role as "the father of lies."[20] Even most theologians, says Father Joseph Komonchak, professor of dogmatic theology at New York's St. Joseph's Catholic Seminary, believe that "a personal devil is something of an embarrassment."[21]

While possessing certain powers, he is not a kind of wicked equal to God. As C. S. Lewis puts it: "The commonest question is whether I really 'believe in the devil.' Now if by 'the devil,' you mean a powerful opposite to God and, like God, self-existent from all eternity, the answer is certainly NO. There is no uncreated being except God. God has no opposite. No being could attain a 'perfect badness' opposite to the perfect goodness of God—the proper question is whether I believe in devils. I do—Satan, the leader or dictator of devils, is the opposite, not of God, but of Michael."[22]

The third trait of Satan is that he is powerful—but not all-powerful.

The New Testament teaches that the world in which we live is under Satan's control and will remain so until Jesus Christ returns to earth to begin His new kingdom and reign. It is no wonder, then, that we are besieged with wars, disease, prejudice, poverty and the many other blights which plague the existence of man. These are not God-created, as many people would have us to believe, but works of Satan through men as they seek after ambition and self-fulfillment outside of almighty God. Lewis comes painfully close to the truth when he says that if we choose to work for Satan, we must accept his wages.

Another facet of the character of Satan is his unrestrained greed and selfishness. In his desire to control creation and to be like God, he was the first to possess those traits—and he is the master of them today. Satan has played to these same traits in fallen man in many different ways. He promises some the power of control over others. He gives others an enormous greed for wealth and prestige that cannot be satisfied. He keeps men's eyes turned away from God and toward their position among other men. He instills the desire to "get ahead" no matter what the cost and no matter who gets trampled on in the process. "Getting and spending we lay waste our powers,"[23] as William Wordsworth so aptly put it. Satan wants man's thoughts and energies turned away from a loving God to a self-centered, egomaniacal human nature.

Perhaps the most deadly trait of Satan is his pride. It was this characteristic which first caused his downfall and which dominates his person today. The ambition of Satan is still to be like God. Couched in his overriding sense of pride is Satan's complete inability to love anyone but himself. Being an entirely egocentric being, he has no concept of love. All that he does, all that he offers mankind, is tied up in his pride, in his desire to control and to be the master.[24]

The characteristic which is totally lacking in Satan's personality is the ability to even comprehend real love. The Bible is clear that eternal love is found only in a loving God who is "not wishing for any to perish but for all to come to repentance."[25] The personification of the love of God is the Person of Jesus Christ. "The Word (Christ) became flesh, and dwelt among us, and we beheld His glory . . . full of grace and truth."[26]

Satan is a very real personality. He has very real power. One day his power and his reign will end. One day Jesus will return to His earth to claim His own and set up the perfect kingdom that man has never known because of sin. At that time, Satan will be chained and cast into a lake of fire.

Helmut Thielicke has stated that when Christ walked this earth the demonic powers gathered themselves together in one last effort to preserve their doomed kingdom. The nearer the returning Christ comes to this aeon, he says, "the more energetically the adversary mobilizes his last reserves, until the demonic excesses reach their climax and the new aeon of God begins."[27]

The Bible is not a fairy tale—it is either right or it is wrong. If it is wrong concerning Christ and Satan, then man has nothing to fear, he can live life as though there were no tomorrow.

But if it is right . . . ?

Perhaps the reality of Satan can best be expressed by one who has been there. Following is the personal experience of Coni, a 24-year-old ex-Satanist from Berkeley, California.[25]

"My involvement in a witch thing came partly as a result of trying to get off drugs. I started reading 'Domains of the Devil.' I already believed in supernatural forces, and Satan seemed like a powerful being to me. The book made sense; I thought what it had to offer would take the place of drugs—and maybe even straighten out my head.

"The dude I was living with knew a witch who had been into it for a long time. She was enthusiastic about my background—felt I could become a 'familiar' under her. Since she was responsible to Elji, a demon of destruction, she was going to teach me to destroy.

"At first it was all memory work. We weren't allowed to get any books on our own. The whole spiritual thing seemed real and exciting. I got insights into why man does things that he does. I began to develop what seemed like a close relationship to Satan. I had a feeling of power to do what he wanted me to do. I wasn't afraid at all. I dug it.

"And besides that, I was off drugs! There were still temptations, but concentration on the new things I was learning kept me from turning on.

"Then came the day of my first black mass. It was

155

a mockery of the Roman Catholic mass. The priest, called the goat, led the assembly in chants and meditations. People performed perverted sexual acts. A girl named Jan sacrificed her baby, burning it alive. And me? I was one of six up for approval by Satan. For a week we had a special herb diet designed to 'dry us out.' Before the mass there was a big dinner of selected foods which made my whole body tingle.

"The whole thing was a big deal—would we make it or not? How I wanted to work for Satan! I was told that when I died, I would be a demon to possess people. The giving of this gift really excited me, and I wanted to die so I could be a demon right away. While I lived, my job was to literally blow people's minds. My witch taught me that the best tool is to get people stoned on drugs and then play games with their heads. She also taught me to hurt people deliberately. I succeeded with one guy named Steve—he's still in a mental hospital.

"It was also my job to get more people into Satan worship. My witch had me as a favorite and got me far into her craft. She laid on me lots of subtle ways to get to people's heads. It was smooth to feel Satan's power.

"Then suddenly one morning everything in my head flashed back to the beautiful people I had known in high school and college. Why was I now trying to destroy people? Suddenly, Satan's power was something I hated. This wasn't it. I took to heroin, a new drug for me, and began riding with the Gypsy Jokers. What I dug about them was their beating up people, raping girls. There lingered a sense of being under Satan's power. I was sort of a backslide demon.

"It was an old high school friend and her husband who caught me off guard. They told me I didn't have to look all my life for new ways to get power. They said God had a much better life for me if I would just take it. The thought of Christianity turned me off, but they shared with me their personal experience with a Person. Jesus Christ wasn't distant and inaccessible like I thought. They talked as if they knew Him. From then on strange things began happening to me, and eventually I asked Jesus to come into my life.

"I lost my appetite for drugs. Two months later reality began to replace fantasy. I felt a new inner strength which enabled me to face life in a way I never had before. God was healing my mind. The hardest thing is to keep from trying to use God's power to meet my own needs. I still have a long way to go."

Thielicke has profoundly stated, "It is not easy to speak of the reality of the demonic powers because this cannot be a mere matter of gathering some biblical passages. As long as we merely proceed thus statistically, *we are not facing the reality of the demonic.*"[29]

Footnotes for Chapter 9

1. Anton La Vey, "The Church of Satan," *McCall's*, March 1970, p. 133.

2. Anton La Vey in "The Church of Satan" by Lance Gilmore in *Man, Myth and Magic*, (Great Britain: Purnell, Inc., 1970), vol. 1, no. 9, p. 270.

3. Hanz Holzer, *The Truth About Witchcraft* (Garden City, N.Y.: Doubleday, 1969), p. 235.

4. Interview with Anton La Vey by Ozwald Guinness, taped lecture "The Encircling Eyes," 1968. L'Abri Fellowship, Huemoz, Switzerland.

5. *Newsweek*, July 19, 1971, p. 22.

6. *Newsweek*, August 16, 1971, p. 56.

7. A.P.I., *Santa Monica Outlook*, July 10, 1970.

8. *Newsweek*, August 16, 1971, p. 56.

9. *Los Angeles Herald Examiner*, December 21, 1969.

10. "Satanism—A Practical Guide to Witch Hunting," *American Opinion* magazine, September 1970, p. 6.

11. "Satanism—A Practical Guide to Witch Hunting," p. 8.

12. Ozwald Guinness, "The Encircling Eyes," alludes to his personal knowledge of the sacrifice of humans in Satanic worship services. Derelicts and prostitutes, he claims, are prime targets for such ritual killings.

13. "Satanism—A Practical Guide to Witch Hunting," p. 9.

14. *Newsweek*, August 16, 1971.

15. C.S. Lewis, *The Problem of Pain* (New York: The Macmillan Co., 1943).

16. McCandlish Phillips, *"The Bible, the Supernatural, and the Jews* (New York and Cleveland: The World Publishing Co., 1970), p. 70.

17. 2 Corinthians 11:14.

18. Ezekiel 28:11-18.

19. Genesis 3.

20. John 8:44.

21. *Newsweek*, August 16, 1971.

22. C. S. Lewis, *The Screwtape Letters* (New York: The Macmillan Co., 1943), p. 4.

23. William Wordsworth, "The World Is Too Much With Us," *The Viking Book of Poetry of the English Speaking World* (New York: Viking Press, 1941), p. 660.

24. Luke 4:1-14.

25. 2 Peter 3:9.

26. John 1:14.

27. Helmut Thielicke, *Man in God's World* (New York: Harper and Row, 1963), translated and edited by J. W. Doberstein.

28. *Focus on Youth*, vol. 4, no. 2, Summer 1970, Young Life, Colorado Springs, Colorado, p. 15.

29. Helmut Thielicke, *Fragen Des Christentums An Die Moderne Welt* (Tubingen: Mohr, 1947), p. 171.

PART FOUR
SPIRITUALISM

"*The man who denies the phenomena of spiritism today is not entitled to be called a skeptic; he is simply ignorant.*"

Jay Hudson, Ph.D., LL.D.
The Law of Psychic Phenomena

CHAPTER 10

That's the Spirit PART 1

James Pike, Jr., was what we might consider an average 20-year-old "student of the world." Disturbed by the hypocrisy that he saw in the "establishment," both in society and in religion, he took the well-trodden road of escape—a path which led him through a tangle of Haight-Ashbury freaks, LSD trips and Cambridge dissidents.

He was a handsome young man with a good amount of intelligence, a very healthy ego and a few odd personality quirks—curious things like a strong dislike for women's bangs and long fingernails. Or a great fondness for warm rooms and sour milk.

The fact that his father was a bishop in the Episcopal Church made communication between the two of them no easier. The bishop, after all, was a busy man and their philosophies of life were so completely different. Plus, the father seemed to have little time or concern for his son. Their life together as father and son didn't really begin until Jim was almost twenty. It ended a short four and a half months later, when Jim shot and killed himself on February 4, 1966.

The communication between the two of them was finished.

Or was it?

The strange story which follows might cause us to take a second look at spiritualism. How else could we interpret the weird events which began to occur just two weeks after Jim's death?

Bishop Pike occupied an apartment near England's Cambridge University with his chaplain, Rev. David Barr; his secretary, Mrs. Maren Begrud, and all the mementos of his late son—whom he had come to love dearly in the last few months. His son's fate had been sealed to his memory just a few short weeks before when Bishop Pike ordered Jim's body cremated and his ashes scattered over the Pacific Ocean.

It was in this Cambridge flat that the series of macabre happenings took place.[1]

The first was the discovery of two of Jim's postcards, purchased prior to his death, found at a 140-degree angle on the floor. Though the trio passed off this incident as insignificant, each was reminded of Jim's love for souvenir cards.

Two days later, the two men noticed that a section of Maren Begrud's bangs had been cut off as if by a pair of scissors. Maren was equally shocked when she looked into a mirror. The following morning another third of Maren's bangs were gone—with no apparent explanation. Bishop Pike and David Barr were dignified men—intellectuals who were far beyond the playing of some childish game or prank.

The next morning, February 24, Maren awoke with a sharp cry of pain. Her third and fourth fingernails had been injured as if a needle had been forced under them. (One nail was actually broken and later fell off.) Still terrified by the painful experience, Maren returned from bandaging her split nail. Upon seeing her, David cried out, "Maren! The rest of your bangs are gone!" And so they were. The game of intrigue was growing out of control. It was also beginning to make some weird kind of sense.

It seems as though Jim Jr. before his death had not only expressed to his father his strong dislike for Maren's bangs but had also informed her that she should cut them off. Jim had finally gotten his way. The bangs were gone.

Maren then revealed an experience she had had the night before. She had tiptoed into the bishop's room to get a book and had witnessed him sitting up in bed speaking trance-like into space. The broken sentences expressed not the bishop's philosophy of life at all but that of his drug-crazed son. "Caring about people is a great mistake . . . you can't count on anybody, and I certainly don't want anybody counting on me. In fact, they can't . . . the only thing that matters is getting what one wants for oneself. If that involves 'using' people, letting them down, getting them out of the way . . . okay! Look out for Number One. That's the only policy. . . ."[2]

This was just the beginning. The unaccountable placement of the postcards, the singed hair, the broken fingernails and the mysterious chatter were followed by over fifty more unexplainable signs indicating to the trio that James Jr. was trying to contact his father.

Strange movements

Bishop Pike had read about "poltergeists" (noisy spirits or ghosts) causing strange phenomena in houses once occupied by a deceased person, but he had never put much stock into these accounts.[3] Now things were different. Each of the three residents began looking for anything which would indicate a further evidence of the late Jim. David quickly noticed that the venetian blinds in the bedroom were unnaturally closed, not in the usual manner but as only Jim would have closed them. The next morning he discovered that all the milk, including that which had been delivered fresh that morning, had gone sour, yet the weather was more than cold enough to keep the milk fresh. Upon learning of the milk incident, the bishop remembered having read that the presence of a witch often made milk curdle and cows run dry.

But there was no "witch" around.

Or was there?

On Sunday evening, February 27, the trio returned to the apartment to find it much too warm. The bishop had checked the thermostat before leaving and distinctly remembered that the house had been cool. The thermostat had been turned down upon their departure. The room was now uncomfortably warm and the temperature gauge was turned on high. This, it seems, was the way Jim had always liked it. In fact, he and his father had often disagreed upon this very issue.

The situation was becoming unbearable. Both the bishop and his chaplain, as well as their secretary, came to dread each day as they anticipated the inevitable find of further "freak" happenings.

It was this unrest that finally led Bishop Pike to Canon John Pearce-Higgins, an acquaintance and vice provost of Southwark Cathedral. Pearce-Higgins had done considerable research on occultism in London, where the Anglican Church's Fellowship and the Society for Psychical Research had extensive files on spiritualist phenomena, in every case substantiating the fact of life after death. After a suggested Ouija board seance had failed to establish communication with his son, Bishop Pike allowed Pearce-Higgins to arrange a seance with the famous British medium, Mrs. Ena Twigg.

The day before the sitting on March 1, there was a veritable onslaught of spiritual phenomena for the bishop and his friends. Closed windows were found open, books were mysteriously moved, clothes misplaced, safety pins scattered about in various places and a broken cigarette was found lying in front of the bishop's nightstand. The cigarette was definite-

167

ly Jim's, since no one else in the flat smoked that particular brand!

The mood was right for what they were about to witness. The three decided that it would be good if they could see something happen before their eyes rather than find it later. Then, as Maren reached into her closet, a silver hand mirror which had been wrapped and stored at the back of the shelf began to move slowly toward the front edge. As the group watched dumbfoundedly, the mirror slithered—not fell—to the floor. The shelf had slanted toward the back of the closet, making such an occurrence impossible by chance.

Three more clues were discovered. First, a lock of blonde, singed hair, unmistakably Maren's, was found in the same spot near the nightstand. Second, a pair of open safety pins unexplainably appeared on the ledge in the bathroom arranged in the now familiar 140-degree angle. And finally, a paperback book was found on the floor with another of Jim's souvenir postcards glued to one of its pages.

The strange angle at which many of the objects had been found remained a mystery until Bishop Pike visualized the hands of a clock at that same angle. The coroner in New York City had fixed the time of Jim's death at approximately 3:00 A.M., New York time. This would be exactly 8:19 A.M. in London—a precise 140-degree angle on the clock!'

And so Bishop Pike, the Episcopalian minister, visited the well-known spiritualist medium, Mrs. Ena Twigg. The home in which she lived and worked was as unpretentious as her contact with the spirit world that afternoon.

Bishop Pike handed Mrs. Twigg Jim's passport (which the bishop had brought with him "just in case"). Mrs. Twigg became suddenly silent. Her body became tense as she announced, "He's here; he's working hard to get through."

A voice speaks

Then she began speaking in the first person. "I failed the test, I can't face you, can't face life. I'm confused . . . very sudden passing . . . have had to do this . . . couldn't find anyone. God, I didn't know what I was doing. But when I got here, I found I wasn't such a failure as I thought. My nervous system failed . . . I am not in purgatory, but something like hell . . . yet nobody blames me here."[5]

The spirit speaking through the medium, Mrs. Twigg continued, "You were under pressure at the same time; I was worried about you, Dad, because they were kicking you around. I came to your room. I moved books . . . I love you very much. . . ."[6]

The reference to "Dad" in the conversation was most convincing to Bishop Pike, since his son had seldom used any other expression in talking with his father. The explanation of the disheveled rooms was further proof, coupled with the allusion to a "golden gate" that Jim was "glad about." Though Mrs. Twigg had no knowledge of the late Jim's cremation, Rev. Pike immediately recognized the comment as referring to his sprinkling of Jim's ashes over the Pacific Ocean beyond the Golden Gate Bridge.

A startling facet of this first seance was the appearance in spirit form of Paul Tillich, the well-known German-American theologian and philosopher who had passed away the previous winter. He and the bishop had been close friends and comrades in their campaigns against many of the orthodox Christian doctrines. Rev. Tillich not only commended the bishop on his firm stand toward liberal theology but thanked him profusely for having dedicated his newest book to him. The book, *What Is This Treasure?*, was barely off the press and had been dedicated to Paul Tillich and John A.T. Robinson, the well-known bishop of the Church of England.

Toward the end of the seance, there appeared to be a great conflict between Jim Pike and Paul Tillich as to who was going to dominate the conversation. Mrs. Twigg at one point found it necessary to rebuke Tillich and insist that only one talk at a time.

When Jim declared that he could not believe in God as a person nor could he be a Christian because he had seen nothing to make him "any more inclined to believe in God," Tillich disagreed. "Well, he hasn't been here very long," he replied, referring to Jim. "I still hold the belief but I now conceive of it somewhat differently."[7]

In a later session with Mrs. Twigg, Bishop Pike asked his son if he had acquired any additional insight into his previous theological comments. "Yes," Jim replied through Mrs. Twigg. "Now I feel there is 'Something.' It's beginning to make sense to assume that Someone is making things hang together and develop . . . but since I've been here, I haven't heard anything about Jesus."[8]

Still another seance by Mrs. Twigg revealed a further elaboration of Jim's on the subject of God and Jesus Christ: "They talk about Jesus as a mystic, a seer, yes, a seer. I haven't met Him. Oh, but Dad, they don't talk about Him as a savior. As an example, you see? Don't you ever believe that God can be personalized. He is the Central Force, and you all give your quota toward it. Do you agree with me, Dad?"[9]

Bishop Pike did.

The next medium with whom the bishop spoke was Rev. George Daisley, an Englishman living in Santa Barbara, California. Rev. Daisley had, at their first meeting, made contact with Edgar Cayce (the famous humanitarian/spiritualist),[10] Bishop Pike's Uncle Bill and Jim Pike himself. In a later seance, Jim spoke through Daisley, saying: "I haven't heard anything personally about Jesus. Nobody around me seems to talk about him. When we come over here, we have a choice, to remain as we are or to grow in our understanding. Some still seem to be church minded and are waiting for a Judgment Day, but these seem to be the unenlightened ones. Others seem to be expanding their mind and self toward more Eastern understandings. I have talked to someone of Chinese origin who offered to help me. He said, 'All of life is a process of evolution and growth.' It seems that the more intellect used, the better. But we're dealing with a 'mind self' which we are fusing with the 'spirit self.' They tell me it will take much endeavor to find the truth."[11]

171

Renewed interest in spiritualism

When asked about Jesus Christ, the spirit stated, "A man came to earth who was Jesus, I am sure, and I would assume he came from the sphere where the purified are. I am in the sphere where those who've made mistakes are, but there seems to be no reason why at some period of eternity we can't all be a part of what some call the 'Christ sphere.' "[12]

The spirit never mentioned salvation from sin through Jesus Christ. Rather, Jim spoke of man "cleansing himself gradually and continuously" as he evolves and becomes more "enlightened." In another seance, contact was made indirectly (through Jim's spirit) with Maren Begrud, Dr. Pike's secretary, who since had committed suicide with an overdose of sleeping pills. She said, "Jesus is just another person . . . been here longer. But I have been told that the people who have been here long enough to advance to a high plane or a high dimension can always come down to a lower plane to help us. But we who are just here have to earn the right to go up."[13]

There it was—enough evidence for Dr. Pike to be totally convinced of life after death. Earthbound spirits, planes of development, rewards for achievement and Jesus a master medium. And equally as impressive was the seemingly proven fact that the dead can and do communicate with the living.

If the attempted communication with his son by Bishop Pike did nothing more than bring a respectable public hearing to spiritualism and spiritualists, it was worth it to fellow spiritualists. A relatively small movement up until the past few years, the ancient religion of spiritualism boasts between 500 and 700 thousand followers in the United States and over 1.5 million around the world.[14] the *raison d'etre* of spiritualism, according to Dr. Marcus Bach (a noted liberal scholar) is the "demonstration and proof of the continuity of life, coupled with the comforting assurance that life is good."[15]

Moving in to fill the gap in the heart of the bereaved seeker, the philosophy of spiritualism assures the living that death is not real but merely a curtain behind which is found life in its fullness. Not two worlds at all, the spiritualist believes there is but one interblended, interrelated world where consciousness and personality cannot die.

The comforting message of eternal bliss for everyone and a reassurance of man's supposed basic goodness are tempting lures into this rather vague pattern of thinking in which man has the prospect of becoming a god. Victor H. Ernest, an ex-spiritualist medium and student of psychic phenomena, relates that according to spiritualist teaching, a person's spiritual development is based largely on his moral and human development while on earth. His own denial of alcohol and cigarettes as well as his improved morals and manners would surely place him on a higher plane than others, the "control spirit" told him.[16] (A "control spirit" is one who is said to speak through the medium during the seance.)

People who live extremely sinful lives would be earthbound spirits when they die, the spiritualist believes. Their assignment to earth would not be permanent, however, as there are at least 18 levels of development upwards to full honors. One spiritualist on TV's "Today Show" reported that as many as "33 planes" have recently been discovered.

"I have always believed in life after death," affirms Dr. Bach, "and the traditional church believes it too. Spiritism went a step further; it asked us to believe that the spirits were interested and active in human affairs, that they could be reached, seen and communicated with. The sense of assurance and comfort lingers (after a seance). The feeling of genuineness persists . . . For those who believe, spiritualism leads to God.""

If spiritualism does lead us to God, as Marcus Bach informs us, then Bishop Pike was on the right track. But if it does not, if it is, in fact, a web of disillusion and half-truths, then the end is worse than the beginning.

How can we know for sure?

Footnotes for Chapter 10

1. The events to follow are enumerated in more detail in James A. Pike and Diane Kennedy's *The Other Side* (New York: Doubleday and Company, Inc., 1968).

2. Pike and Kennedy, *The Other Side*, pp. 87, 88.

3. Hanz Holzer, the parapsychologist, claims in his book, *The Truth About Witchcraft* (New York: Doubleday, 1969) that he knows personally of occasions where poltergeists (or ghosts) have turned light switches on and off in full view of the owners of the house (Dr. Samuel Kahn, a psychiatrist) and also of an instance in which a carving knife rose and slowly descended in an arc to the feet of a naval architect and his wife. Other such phenomena are reported in many of Holzer's other works including *ESP and You, Ghost Hunter, Ghosts I've Met,* and *Lively Ghosts of Ireland.*

4. Experiences such as the bishop's stopped clock are not at all unusual. Mr. Edmond P. Gibson, a student at the parapsychological laboratory, relates a most intriguing episode in the life of the late Dr. John F. Thomas, wherein the plug of Gibson's office clock was pulled out from the wall socket at the precise minute Dr. Thomas was killed in an auto accident miles away. For more than a decade prior, Thomas had been receiving "messages" from his deceased wife, Ethel. In hundreds of similar case studies, the widowed mate is usually led into further attempts at communicating with the deceased partner. Martin Ebon, *True Experiences in Communicating With the Dead* (New York: Signet, 1968), p. 59.

5. Pike and Kennedy, *The Other Side,* p. 115.

6. Pike and Kennedy, *The Other Side,* p. 115.

7. Pike and Kennedy, *The Other Side,* p. 128.

8. James A. Pike and Diane Kennedy, *The Other Side* (New York: Dell Publishing Co., 1968), p. 133.

9. Pike and Kennedy, *The Other Side,* p. 282, 283, 324.

10. For an excellent analysis of the life and writings of Edgar Cayce from a Christian perspective, read James Bjornstad, *Twentieth Century Prophecy* (Minneapolis: Bethany Fellowship, 1969).

11. Pike and Kennedy, *The Other Side* (Dell edition), p. 187.

12. Pike and Kennedy, *The Other Side,* p. 187.

13. Pike and Kennedy, *The Other Side,* p. 282.

14. Walter R. Martin, *The Kingdom of the Cults* (Minneapolis: Bethany Fellowship, 1965), p. 199.

15. Marcus Bach in *The Kingdom of the Cults,* p. 199.

16. See Victor H. Ernest, *I Talked With Spirits* (Wheaton: Tyndale House, 1970), pp. 25, 26, 72. Also Jan K. Van Baalen, *Chaos of the Cults* (Grand Rapids: Eerdmans, 1962), Spiritism section, pp. 33, 34.

17. Marcus Bach in *Kingdom of the Cults,* p. 199.

> *"Do you know how exciting it is to come back? . . . I want so much to tell you about a world where everybody is out to create a greater sense of love and harmony."*

> Jim Pike, Jr. (after death)
> through Mrs. Ena Twigg

CHAPTER 11

That's the Spirit PART 2

Sir Arthur Conan Doyle acclaimed spiritualism as "the greatest revelation the world has ever known!"[1]

A most generous testimonial, indeed, considering the fraud and fakery which surrounded the early days of modern spiritualism.

It all began in December of 1847 when John and Margarete Fox together with their two younger children, Margaretta and Katie, moved into the modest frame house near Hydesville, New York.[2] Though there had been rumors to the effect that the house was haunted, John Fox, a Methodist farmer, was unimpressed. Until the night of March 31, 1848, that is, when Katie (then age 12) heard the now familiar rapping and thumping in her room and suddenly called out the words that were to mark the beginning of modern spiritualism: "Here, Mr. Splitfoot, do as I do!"

Mr. Splitfoot apparently not only heard young Katie, but responded by counting out the children's ages as well as answering questions with a rapping for "yes" and silence for "no." Soon an alphabet system was established and it was learned that the communiques were emanating from the ghost of a peddler named Charles Rosna who had been murdered by a previous tenant. Later, the Foxes dug up their cellar and found relics of Charles' hair, teeth and bones. Of course, no proper examination was made of these artifacts, lest the immediate popularity of the Fox family disappear.

Mrs. Ann Leah Fish of Rochester, Margaretta's married sister, soon got in on the action and the "mysterious" rappings spread to every city visited by the family members. So popular was this unique "thumping," in fact, that within three years there were more than one hundred mediums in New York City and more than fifty seance groups meeting regularly in Philadelphia.

But "easy come, easy go" as the proverb says.

For after a public seance in Buffalo in 1851, three medical doctors exposed the Fox-Splitfoot-Rosna "seances" and denounced the rappings as a fraud. The investigators explained that the noises had been produced by the cracking of the knee joints—

a fact which was soon afterwards admitted by the girls. Furthermore, Margaretta and Katie explained that they had both mastered the art of "toe-cracking." The girls were self-styled charlatans who had gladly taught their lucrative "trade" to any who were interested.

Had the girls the integrity to announce their prank earlier, it would have been enough simply to dismiss the entire hoax as the thoughtless yet harmless play of two not-so-naive youngsters. But it was not left there. The greedy and amoral duet had continued their devious "seances" and in so doing given false hope to many bereaved men and women. Capitalizing on the grief of widows and mothers who had just lost their children, the sisters had turned their invention into a profitable but disgusting vocation. By the time of their admission of guilt the spiritualist movement was raging out of control.

So began the "greatest revelation the world has ever known."

Is it really? Or could the *greatest* revelation have come not through the Fox sisters, nor through Arthur Ford, nor through Ena Twigg but through the written and spoken word of God Himself?

"In the beginning was the Word," we are told by John in his Gospel record, "and the Word was with God, and the Word was God. . . . glory as of the only begotten from the Father, full of grace and truth."[3]

What was this "Word" which was from the beginning? The ancient Greeks had a special way of describing the expression of the Almighty. The term was *logos* or "the Word." *Logos* involved the concept of the ultimate purpose or reason behind the universe. It meant, in effect, the "Last Word." This expression is used of Jesus Christ to express the thought of the full communication of God to man.

Jesus Christ was and is the "Last Word." "There is one mediator between God and men, the man Christ Jesus."[4] He alone stands in the gap created by man's rejection of God.

Some would have us erroneously believe that the proof of eternal life originated with spiritualism. A recent issue of *Psychic* magazine, for instance, features an article on "20th century proof" of life after death.[5] Such thinking reveals an ignorance of the religious history of man (such as the purpose behind many ancient cave drawings). From earliest times, man has been aware of a future life past his earthbound existence. This awareness was placed in man by God so that His creation would look to Him for eternal spiritual life.

Death is no mystery to the person who understands the message of the Bible. To the true Christian, there is no fear of death or dying.[6] The record of Scripture was written so that we "may believe that Jesus is the Christ, the Son of God; and that believing you may have life in His Name."[7]

The Scriptures clearly teach that the way to God is not through mediums or seers but through faith in the only Son of God. He stands alone in His claim to be "the way, and the truth, and the life."[8]

This being the case, if Christ is the only mediator between God and man, how does one explain the mystical phenomena which accompany spiritualism?

180

Seances

We might begin by trying to understand what actually takes place at a seance. The first step in any true seance is the trance. Often preceded by the Lord's Prayer or another prayer directed to God the Father, the trance is an unconscious state of mind into which the medium places himself. Silence is requested, and often necessary, as any outside disturbance might distract his concentration. (Mr. Victor Ernest during his early childhood would practice blotting out all conscious thought from his mind for several minutes a night. Eventually he could sit for fifteen to twenty minutes a night without being distracted by a single conscious thought.)⁹

After the medium has lapsed into a trance, a foreign spirit takes control. Using the vocal chords of the medium, the "control" spirit will completely empower any verbal pronouncements. The voice which emits from the medium's mouth is usually either slightly higher or lower in tone than that of the medium.

The job of the "control" spirit, spiritualists believe, is either to offer a message himself to those present or else to introduce another spirit to speak —called a "familiar spirit." According to spiritualist teaching, this would be the spirit of the deceased individual in question. The familiar spirit would then speak in the first person in an audible voice, closely resembling that of the deceased.

In the case of Arthur Ford, "Fletcher" was the name of the control spirit who had worked with him and through him since 1924 to present a message from "the other side." (Ethel Meyers, another reputable medium, has "Albert," the supposed spirit of her deceased husband, as her "control.") As soon as contact is made with the "familiar" spirit the "control" spirit is thought to leave the scene.

There is a great question in the minds of spiritualists as to whether or not all departed spirits (familiar) are able to make a vocal appearance through a medium. (For example, it was impossible to speak with Mrs. Maren Begrud through medium George Daisley until the spirit of Jim Pike interceded for her.)

In the majority of cases where true spiritualism is involved, the party desirous of communicating with the deceased is forced to accept or reject the validity of the seance on the basis of the truth of the information relayed through the medium. This is due to the fact that the seeker is rarely allowed to hear the spirit speak audibly himself but only through the mouth of the medium.[10]

The authenticity of the received message can be tested in several ways. A revelation of facts about the deceased which were previously unknown to the medium, a peculiar mannerism in speaking or the use of certain "key" words or phrases are usually the bases on which the authenticity of a seance can be verified. On the basis of this information, the seeker should be in a position to accept the contact with a spirit as being real or reject it as foolishness.

Let's create an example. If I wanted to speak with my deceased father, I could seek out a medium who would probably fit into one of three categories. Either this "seer" would be a complete phony, or he would be a sincere individual with a keen sensitivity to extrasensory perception or else he could actually be used as a vehicle for supernatural conveyance.

In the case of the first "medium," it is usually not too hard to spot fraud, as we have previously shown. But between the second and third there is often a fine line of separation. Numerous parapsychological tests have proven that certain individuals are born with more acute sensitivity to thought transference than others (i.e., mind reading and ESP)." These persons are not to be confused with those who align themselves with an outside power and serve only as a relay of that power. Whereas those with ESP have control over their psychic powers and exercise them consciously, those in the third category have no control over the independent use of their faculties and are nearly always oblivious to the messages they convey.

Let us assume that I spotted the faker and went on to the remaining two "professionals." The first would be able to tell me no more about my father than I already knew (though the information may have been stored in my subconscious mind). This reading (often termed "mental telepathy"), when tempered with known facts and a lot of common sense, could be very deceiving were the psychic to attribute it to spirit communication. The third man would be the only genuine spiritualist in the accepted sense of the word. When in a trance, the medium in this case would serve as nothing more than a terminal or station between the transmitting supernatural agency and the receiving human being.

Very often the genuine medium also has developed psychic ability in addition to his capacity for relaying spirit messages. Such could very well have been the case with Rev. Arthur Ford. Though some of the information Ford relayed during his televised seance with Bishop Pike and Allen Spraggett could be accounted for as ESP, the citing of information unknown to either Pike or Spraggett would tend to place the occurrence into the third category—that of spirit communication.

Such could also have been the case with Diane Kennedy, Bishop Pike's wife (whom he married in 1968), when she saw a vision of the death of her husband and his ascension into heaven. Several days after her husband's death in the Judean desert, she reportedly witnessed him leaving his body in a filmy, cloud-like substance which rose slowly between two rocks up toward the brim of a canyon. Though the filmy apparition was otherwise featureless, Diane insists she remembers her late husband smiling and thereby being reassured with a feeling of deep peace. Similar visions of the bishop wandering in the wilderness were observed by Ford and others who comforted the bereaved Mrs. Pike with their belief in eternal life and the continuous existence of the spirit.

For countless thousands throughout the world, these visions added fuel to the flame of spiritualist teaching. Bishop Pike had died and communication with the spirit world was established. Several different well-known spiritualists received similar visions and communications from the other side. Therefore what they saw was to be believed as a reasonable explanation of spirit phenomena.

Or was it?

Here is where the real deception of spiritualism comes into focus. It is logical to assume that if there is true communication from the spirit world, that communication will be correct because it is "spiritual." This assumes that there are only pure spirits and leaves no room for evil spirit beings.[12] This is quite an assumption in light of the Word of God, as we shall see.

To assume that the source of all spirit communication is a perfect being or beings is to deny the true picture of the spirit world as presented in the Word of God. The Bible reveals that there are evil spirits, or demons, present throughout our world and carrying out their mission—often that of peace and goodwill.[13]

"For our struggle is not against flesh and blood," the apostle Paul warns us, "but against the rulers, against the powers, against the world-forces of this darkness, against the spiritual forces of wickedness in the heavenly places."[14] Far from being pure and innocent, the unseen spiritual world is a battleground of wicked, self-willed spirit beings mixed together with powerful, God-directed spirits of light.[15]

An advantage which the evil spirits who inhabit our world have over mankind is that they do not *appear* to be evil. Their facade is a masquerade of truth, beauty and goodness. Satan, we are told by the apostle Paul, disguises himself as an angel of light and "therefore it is not surprising if his servants also disguise themselves as servants of righteousness."[16] Satan cleverly deceives the minds of those who seek truth and splashes his brilliance before their eyes to the extent that their minds are darkened to the truth of God—"the light of the gospel of the glory of Christ."[17]

There are two major errors into which those who follow spiritualism fall. The first is that the "control spirit" is an honest, truthful spirit—which he is not. The second is that the "familiar spirit" is the spirit of the dead person (or that person in spirit form)— which cannot possibly be true.

It is sheer nonsense to believe that the spirit of a person leaves his body upon death and is left to float about aimlessly, or be summoned to some spirit depository to be called at will by another spirit to speak to the living. This fantasy of vapor visions, soul travel and disembodied spirits belongs in the realm of Disneyland—not in religion texts.

Due to the superstitious bent of the human mind and man's natural inclination toward idolatry, it is not surprising to find that nearly every nation in the Old Testament which turned its back on God was also deeply involved in spiritualism.

The nation of Israel was *the* exception. As God's people, they were forbidden to have any dealings whatsoever with mediums. Attempted communication between the living and the dead was to be shunned at all expense. The penalty for such disobedience to the commandment of God was death by stoning.[18]

The reason for such stringent penalty was basic. God knew that spiritualism was an aberration of the truth designed by Satan to deceive men into believing a lie, thereby distracting them from their worship of the only true God.

The witch of Endor

In 1 Samuel 28, the Old Testament relates the story of King Saul and the medium of Endor. After following the Lord's commandment to banish all seers and mediums from the land, Saul went back on his own edict and sought a woman "that had a familiar spirit."[19] This most unwise decision on the part of Saul was made after God had apparently refused to answer him regarding the destiny of Israel because of Saul's prior disobedience. The holy prophet Samuel, who often spoke God's words to Saul, had died. Saul and his army were facing the mighty forces of the Philistines—and Saul was afraid. He had no assurance of victory in the upcoming battle . . . because he had no word from God.

In desperation, wanting to know the outcome of the battle before it began, Saul sent his servants out to seek a medium. Disguised as a commoner, Saul then made his visit after dark to the medium's house. His purpose? To communicate with the departed spirit of Samuel in order to discern what he should do in the battle against the Philistines.

When the woman actually saw a spirit coming up out of the earth, she screamed and realized that it was King Saul who had tricked her into conducting the seance. Upon his insistence, she continued the sitting by revealing that she saw an "old man covered with a mantle."[20] King Saul exclaimed that it was

Samuel and then proceeded to ask him what should be his battle tactics against the Philistines.

The spirit swore to Saul that because he had transgressed God's law, he would die in the battle and that the following day Saul and his sons would be with him (Samuel). The spirit vanished, and Saul fell exhausted on the ground.

Saul disregarded the fact that the Lord is God. And he paid the price of his disobedience. The prophecy was correct. The Philistines overran Israel and Saul committed suicide on the battlefield.

But where did Saul get his information? A mentally disturbed woman, perhaps? The real Samuel returned from the dead? Or perhaps an evil spirit imitating Samuel?

These three views are all held by various scholars and theologians. The first, however, must be ruled out on the grounds that "those with familiar spirits" (mediums) were prevalent throughout that period of history. Rulers of surrounding nations put an enormous value on the advice of seers, mediums and necromancers. King Saul was certainly smarter than to risk his own reputation as king by consulting a mentally-disturbed woman. But if that is not the case, what actually happened at Endor?

There are those who sincerely believe that God intervened in the seance at Endor allowing the real Samuel to be brought back from the dead. Such scholars rest their evidence on the lone fact that the medium was startled at what she saw and (because of Samuel's appearance) recognized Saul as being the king. (Those of this persuasion will quickly admit that this is a highly unusual phenomenon, never again repeated in the Bible.)

Here, however, is perhaps a more logical and feasible explanation. The appearance of Samuel was an impersonation by an evil spirit in the same way that every spirit contact at a seance is made with an evil, deceiving spirit. We must remember that Saul never actually saw the face of Samuel. He did not even speak to him directly. The meager description of an old man covered with a mantle could have fit thousands of old men who had died, as the mantle (or cloak) was worn by nearly every man of that day. It was Saul who jumped to the conclusion that this was Samuel.

The speaking was done, I believe, by a deceiving spirit through the medium. The prediction relayed by the spirit impersonating Samuel in no way necessitated God's involvement. It was an assumption that was generally accepted as being inevitable by most of the people of that day who knew the overwhelming strength of the Philistine army. A prophecy of impending disaster and doom was only logical in light of the circumstances—and if this information was common knowledge among the people, how much more so among the evil spirits.

If God did actually bring back Samuel from the dead, we might well ask ourselves what would prevent Him from doing the same thing again. And again. And again. God has never used the seance to communicate with the living. And when He rejects man's way of reaching Him, He makes no exceptions.[21]

The impact of the story, however, comes not in

the *modus operandi* of the seance but in the reason for its necessity. The Bible tells us that "when Saul inquired of the Lord, the Lord did not answer him. . . . Then said Saul unto his servants, 'Seek for me a woman who is a medium, that I may go to her and inquire of her.' "[22]

Here lies the real problem. King Saul was out of fellowship with his Creator because of his sin and took what he thought was the "easy way out." Rather than confessing his sins to God and allowing Him to heal the breach between them, he sought the reassurance of a spirit being who was less than God. And for this he died.[23]

The reason that the Christian rejects the possibility of spirits of the dead returning to earth is based on the biblical view of death. The Bible clearly teaches that death is a final departure of the soul and spirit of man from his physical body. It is impossible to stage a re-run or make a second try at it. We are born, we live, we die (physically). The soul lives on—but not on earth.

"It is appointed for men to die once, and after this comes judgment."[24] The one who entrusts his life to Jesus Christ has His promise that he will be with his Lord upon death. The belief that one's spirit can return from the dead contradicts the truth of the Word of God regarding man's final destiny. When the Christian dies, his spirit is present immediately with the Lord. When a non-Christian dies, his spirit awaits final judgment.[25] Jesus Christ taught that after a non-Christian dies there is a "great chasm" fixed so that "none may cross over" from their permanent abode in hades.[26]

190

If there is, then, no second chance, no return from the dead, what is it that is heard and often observed at a true seance?

The message that comes through the medium is from a lying, counterfeit spirit. Fulfilling his role as the "father of lies,"[27] Satan sends a deceiving spirit (what the spiritualist would term a "familiar") to bring false comfort and encouragement to the bereaved and to convince them that life beyond the grave is happy without Jesus Christ. In some cases, the spirit is able to relay genuine information about the deceased which is unknown to the medium. In other cases, the spirit mimics the deceased. In no way, though, is the spirit that of the deceased. The biblical term "familiar" is appropriate because the lying is familiar with the deceased individual. The speech, mannerisms and idiosyncrasies of the deceased are aped by the false spirit to the extent that he can easily pass himself off as the dead person.

There is no doubt but that this counterfeit spirit is a *created being*, not a disembodied spirit. According to the Word of God, all spirit beings (including Satan) were originally created by God for the sole purpose of praising the triune God and ruling with Him. Not satisfied with their position as servants, some of these spirits followed Lucifer, "the son of the morning," (now called Satan, or "adversary") in his rebellion against God. The book of The Revelation suggests that up to one third of the angelic beings sided with Lucifer and were cast to earth with him.[28] The earth then became Satan's territory. He is repeatedly designated as the "ruler of this world,"[29] the "world forces of this darkness"[30] and the "prince of the power of the air."[31] Jesus Christ, speaking to John in a vision, confirms the fact that Satan's throne is in the world,[32] to such a degree, in fact that we are told "the whole world lies in the power of the evil one."[33]

It is no wonder, then, that these fallen angels can disguise themselves as spirits of the dead. The confused mind is a playground for evil spirits.[34]

Apports

The existence of the false spirits can be seen in ways other than mere audible communication (i.e., in a seance). The movement of objects such as the rearrangement of the books and postcards in Bishop Pike's apartment is an example of such a nonverbal phenomenon. The items were peculiarly placed by a spirit being—but not the spirit of the late Jim. These and similar phenomena, termed "apports," suggest that objects can be moved through space at the will of the spirits. (The January 25, 1945 issue of the *Psychic Observer* presents an account of an apport in which the control spirit transferred a book from a shelf to a desk three thousand miles away. There is no positive verification of these events, but it is certainly not beyond the "prince of the power of the air" or his spiritual forces.)

Spirit writing

The medium places himself under the control of the spirit world. Placing a pen or pencil in his hand, he relaxes his arm and lapses into a trance. Though the majority of what might be called "spirit writing" today is mere trickery and illusion, there is sufficient uncertainty about many documented incidents to place it into the category of spiritism.[35]

Materializations

In such instances a visible form appears from nowhere and vanishes in like manner. Ectoplasm, a filmy, quasi-material substance present in all human bodies, flowed from the body of Bishop Pike during his wife's vision.[36] The same substance (thought by some to be the conversion of psychic energy into matter through spirit activity) may take the form of a complete body or any part of the body, such as a hand or a face. Several sources claim to "document" such materializations with photographs and scientific corroboration (though such "proof" has been questioned by non-spiritualists).

Ouija board

Perhaps the most widely used device for spirit contact is the *Ouija board*—an antiqued flat board inscribed with the letters of the alphabet and a yes and no circle. In using the Ouija board, the two participants sit facing each other with their knees touching and the board resting on their laps. With their eyes shut and fingertips resting on a triangular indicator, the participants have been instructed that the indicator will move over the letters to spell out a message from the spirit world.

But it's just a gag, you say. Exactly what I

thought as a young college student when a religion professor warned our class against becoming involved with the Ouija board.

On numerous occasions, though, I would talk to people who had become interested in the Ouija and claimed that it had worked for them. So I too joined the ranks of those who bought the board "just to prove it didn't work."

I have since learned that my experience is not the final criterion for evaluating reality. The Ouija board does work—but not for everyone. An interesting point is that in every case where people believe in the power of the Ouija board, you will find a good percentage of correct predictions and answers, whereas with people who disbelieve, the error factor is nearly 100 percent. The reason for this, I conclude, is that the supernatural world is encountered in the final analysis through faith, not merely through human reason. As it requires faith in God through Jesus Christ for man to live in true spiritual union with God, so it requires faith to align oneself with the evil spirits—spirits which cause the triangle to glide across the face of the Ouija board.

The reason for the popularity of the Ouija board is not at all surprising. It can work. The principle is elementary: when the user clears his mind of all conscious thoughts and anticipates an answer to his question, he becomes sensitized to the extrasensory world. Often the answer will come from deep within his subconscious, but frequently the information is totally foreign to the user. In such cases, there is the definite possibility of an evil spirit transmitting the desired information through the unconscious movement of the person's fingertips.[37] (Of interest at this point are the numerous testimonies of those who have asked the Ouija board about the source of its power. The answer invariably denies any connection with the God of the Bible—and often answers with either blasphemy or terms like "Satan," "Father of lies," "God of this world," "Deceiver," or something similar.)

The ease with which a Ouija board can be procured, coupled with an inherent fascination to the novice, makes it one of the most deadly of all the spiritualist "devices." The operator of a Ouija board is easy prey for evil spirits.

In addition to their denial of the existence of evil spirits, spiritualists refute the biblical teaching regarding the role and authority of Jesus Christ. The spirit speaking through the mediums which Bishop Pike encountered, for example, stated that Jesus Christ was not the Saviour of the world. First John 2:22 tells us, "Who is the liar but the one who denies that Jesus is the Christ? This is the antichrist, the one who denies the Father and the Son." In the admission by the "familiar spirit" that there is no Saviour, we find one of the strongest evidences that spirits which speak through mediums are Satan-controlled, since Satan is interested primarily in convincing men that Jesus is not the Son of God and that the Bible is not the Word of God.[38]

A third criticism of spiritualism is that the supposed "spirits of departed souls" usually give evidence of even less understanding than the person they represent. Dr. Koch relates the following example. "A Christian family, members of an evangelical church, hold seances together with their aunt acting as medium. In this way some of the well-known Christians of the past have apparently appeared and conducted the meeting, as well as preached to them. It is noteworthy, though that these 'spirit' sermons contain nothing exceptional and usually fall well below the standard set by the writings of the men in question." If one were actually to contact the spirit of Paul, for example, it would be expected that he would have even greater insights as a spirit than he had as a human. But this is very rarely the case, as Koch illustrates.[39]

The strongest objection to spiritualism is found in the command of God, "Do not turn to mediums or spirits; do not seek them out to be defiled by them. I am the Lord your God."[40] Spiritualism forces one to take his eyes off the Almighty Creator God and look to lesser spirits for the answers to life—and death. It gives credit where credit is not *due,* for the Bible teaches that only God holds all the secrets of the universe and only He can divulge them.

Results of spiritualism

The dangers of spiritualism are pointed out by Professor Bender of the University of Freiburg, "Thousands of people put their hopes in the deceptive proclamations of spiritistic practitioners, receive advice from the other side, and become dependent upon it. I have seen a number of patients who have suffered serious psychic disturbances through the misuse of such practices. They have become split personalities. The spirits which they called confused them. *He who tries to discover the promises of the other side through superstition endangers himself to fall prey to the dark side of his psyche.*"[41]

"Mediumistic psychosis" is the name given to the symptoms of a split personality produced by prolonged activity with mediumistic forces. According to Dr. Koch, strong depression, melancholia, psychopathic disorders and severe psychoses are frequently the results of involvement with spiritualism. Some studies show that suicide is common in occult circles and that psychic disturbances are often passed on to the third and fourth generations.[42]

The probability of contact with impostor spirits is so great, especially in spiritualism, that the apostle John warns his readers, "Do not believe every spirit, but test the spirits to see whether they are from God."[43]

Suffice it to say that spirit involvement is dangerous practice. Exposure to seances and spirit communication, even on a casual level, opens the door for further susceptibility to the possibility of control by evil spirits.

What is the test that a Christian can use to discern whether a spirit is from God or from Satan? "Every spirit that confesses that Jesus Christ has does not confess Jesus is not from God . . ."[44]

There it is. To "confess Jesus Christ has come in the flesh" means to agree that He was both God and man. *"Jesus"* was His human name, given by

197

come in the flesh is from God, and every spirit that
Mary and Joseph. *Christ* was His divine name,
meaning "the Messiah," the promised Saviour. In
the Early Church, when one "confessed Jesus
Christ," he accepted the fact that Christ was the
Son of God and his personal Saviour, thereby com-
mitting himself to this truth.[45] (Conversely, to deny
Jesus Christ was to openly repudiate any allegiance
to Him or His teachings. Repeatedly before the
Roman tribunals, citizens were asked to deny Jesus
Christ, thereby accepting Rome as their authori-
tarian head.)

In his book *I Talked With Spirits*, Victor Ernest
gives testimony to the source of spiritualism.[46] Having been involved with mediumship for some time,
he was disturbed by the verse 1 John 4:3—to the
point that he asked several revealing questions of
the control spirit during an actual seance.

"Do you believe that Jesus was the Son of God?"
he asked the spirit.

"Of course, my child, Jesus is the Son of God.
Only believe as the Bible says," replied the spirit
(through the medium).

"Do you believe that Jesus is the Saviour of the
World?" he asked more specifically.

Avoiding the question, the spirit replied, "My
child, why do you doubt? Why do you not believe?
You have been this long with us: why do you continue to doubt?" Then the spirit began quoting
Scripture about believing.

The third and last question Ernest asked was
"Oh, spirit, you believe that Jesus is the Son of God,
that He is the Saviour of the world. Do you believe

that Jesus died on the cross and shed His blood for the remission of sin?"

The medium was catapulted off his chair. Falling onto the floor in the middle of the living room, he lay groaning as if in deep pain.

The question was settled. The control spirit could not confess to the fact that Jesus Christ had appeared "to seek and to save that which was lost."[47]

So the child of God has given the acid test to apply in order to "try the spirits." It is not based on the emotions of the one receiving the message, nor upon the truthfulness of the message itself. It is based solely on the explicit instruction in the Word of God.

By this test, spiritualism fails to meet God's standard of divine revelation. The mainstream teaching of spiritualism places its followers into the category of those who have fallen away from the faith, "paying attention to deceitful spirits and doctrines of demons."[48] Spiritualism has repeatedly been proven to be totally opposed to God's plan and purpose for His creation. We cannot take lightly that about which God has spoken so strongly.

The prophet Isaiah did a good job of summing it up when he said, "And when they shall say unto you, 'Consult the mediums and the wizards who whisper and mutter,' should not a people consult their God?"[49]

If they speak not according to the word of the Law and the Testimony of Scripture, Isaiah reminds us "it is because they have no dawn (light)."[50]

The Father loves us and wants to communicate

with us. He wants to reveal many of the secrets of His work and His world, but He does so not through mediums and spirits, but through His Son, Jesus Christ.

Christianity stands diametrically opposed to spiritualism for the following reasons:

1. Spiritualism refuses to acknowledge the existence of two types of spirit beings, "evil" as well as "good" spirits (demons and angels).

2. Spiritualism contradicts the teachings of the Bible regarding death, eternal life, the saving power of Jesus Christ and other vital biblical doctrines.

3. Spiritualism often contradicts itself in that the supposed "departed spirits" never sound as intelligent as when they were physically alive. Yet spiritualism teaches that after death a process of perfection is instituted—which would suggest that departed spirits should be able to communicate even more intelligently.

Spiritualism places a reliance upon spirits other than God and in so doing violates the first and greatest commandment, "You shall have no other gods before Me."[51]

In one of his most profound poems, T. S. Eliot strips the heart of man naked of all its embellishments: "We are the hollow men, we are stuffed men leaning together, head piece filled with straw," he proclaims.[52] Such an epitaph should be written across every advertisement for spiritualistic practices.

I'm reminded of the two women who stood at the Lord's open tomb in shocked amazement after His crucifixion. They saw that He was gone . . . immediately two men appeared near them and lovingly asked them the question that should be directed to every devotee and practitioner of spiritualism:

"Why do you seek the living One among the dead?"[53]

Footnotes for Chapter 11

1. Sir Arthur Conan Doyle in Walter R. Martin, *The Kingdom of the Cults* (Minneapolis: Bethany Fellowship, 1965), p. 210.

2. "Spiritualism," *American Heritage,* February, 1971, pp. 34, 35.

3. John 1:1,14.

4. 1 Timothy 2:5.

5. *Psychic* magazine (San Francisco: The Bolen Company), August, 1971, pp. 4-13, 18-23, 26ff.

6. 1 Corinthians 15:55.

7. John 20:31.

8. John 14:6.

9. Victor H. Ernest, *I Talked With Spirits* (Wheaton, Tyndale House, 1970), pp. 17, 18.

10. In a few cases, the medium will assist the seeker(s) in visualizing their own apparition. At such seances, the participants might be instructed to close their eyes, press their thighs together, take long breaths, and imagine a shining light which would then become larger and more distinct until they visualized the person in question.

11. E.R. Dodds records such testing in "Psychical Research Today," *Man, Myth and Magic* (Great Britain: Purnell, Inc., 1970) vol. 1, no. 9, pp. 241-244.

12. Jan Karel Van Baalen, *The Chaos of the Cults* (Grand Rapids: Wm. B. Eerdmans Publishing Co., 1962), pp. 58, 59 cites the testimony of two spiritualists:

"All spirits in the other world are nothing else but the souls that have lived here." (Lanslots, *Spiritualism Unveiled*, p. 36.)

"If for convenience we designate the high ranks (of the departed) *angels*, and the lower as *evil spirits*, let us be careful not to lose sight of the fact that they differ only as elder and younger." (G.G. Andre, *Spiritualism Unveiled*. p. 36.)

13. See Jude 6; Matthew 25:41; Luke 10:17.

14. Ephesians 6:12.

15. See Matthew 4:11; 2 Peter 2:11.

16. 2 Corinthians 11:14,15.

17. 2 Corinthians 4:3,4; John 12:40.

18. See Leviticus 19:31, 20:6,27; Deuteronomy 18:10-12; 1 Chronicles 10:13.

19. 1 Samuel 28:7.

20. 1 Samuel 28:14.

21. An excellent defense of this position is given by Hanson, Bavinck, Orr, and Honig, *Handbook V.D. Geref. Dogmatiek* (Kampen, 1938), p. 796 quoting extensively from the eighteenth-century Dutch theologian P. van Mastricht. In summation:

1. Neither the woman nor her control spirit had power over Samuel. God had. But He refused to answer Saul (v. 6); surely, He would not answer him now that Saul took refuge to forbidden means, least of all by doing a thing He has never been know to duplicate.

2. The true Samuel would not have lied, by saying that Saul had disturbed his rest, if not Saul but God had ordered him.

3. After rejecting Saul for the sin of disobedience and subsequently ignoring him for years, God would not at the last moment

   a. have catered to Saul's desire to receive another revelation;
   b. have acted contrary to the convicion He has always impressed upon His people, namely, that there is no contact between the living and the dead (Job 7:10; Ecclesiastes 9:6; Isaiah 63:16; Luke 16:31);
   c. have created the impression that seeking information from the dead is not so bad, since elsewhere He has commanded this sin to be punished with death *(all spiritists appeal to this passage)*;
   d. have stated that Saul had to die because of this thing in which God yielded to his request (1 Chronicles 10:13).

4. The woman was afraid:

   a. Because in her reading of her visitor's mind she recognized it was Saul, a mighty enemy of mediums or
   b. Because she saw spirits hover above the apparition, who with "lying wonders" (2 Thessalonians 2:9) impersonated Samuel.

22. 1 Samuel 28:6,7.

23. 1 Chronicles 10:13.

24. Hebrews 9:27.

25. 1 Thessalonians 4:14-17.

26. Luke 16:19-31 (especially v. 26).

27. John 8:44.

28. Revelation 12:4; Ezekiel 28:17.

29. John 12:31; 14:30; 16:11.

30. Ephesians 6:12.

31. Ephesians 2:2.

32. Revelation 2:13.

33. 1 John 5:19.

34. See 1 Corinthians 14:33; 2 Timothy 1:7.

35. For an actual sample of "spirit writing" see Ernest, *I Talked With Spirits*, pp. 23, 24.

36. Hanz Holzer, *The Psychic World of Bishop Pike* (New York: Crown Publishers, Inc., 1970), pp. 124-130. (Cf. *The Haunting of Bishop Pike* by Merrill Unger.)

37. The Ouija board can generally be classified under "spirit writing" or "automatic writing." Of this phenomenon, the parapsychologist Rudolf Tischner writes, "We must warn that one must not yield himself unreservedly to this fascinating business . . . else it can reach such a pass that one is no longer master over his own body but a servant, a slave who must obey if he would not meet the very unpleasant results of refusal." (*Ergebnisse Okkulter Forschung*, Deutsche Verlagsanstalt, Stuttgart, 1951, Table of Contents.)

38. 1 John 4:3.

39. The philosopher Wundt once said, "The great minds must have turned into imbeciles at their passing into eternity because they speak such dull and trivial stuff when they are cited by medias (mediums)." Kurt Koch, D.D., *Between Christ and Satan* (Berghausan BD. Germany, Evangelization Publishers, 1961), p. 132.

40. Leviticus 19:31.

41. Professor Bender in *Between Christ and Satan*, p. 153.

42. Koch, *Between Christ and Satan*, pp. 153-166.

43. 1 John 4:1.

44. 1 John 4:2,3.

45. 1 John 2:2; 4:10,14.

46. Ernest, *I Talked With Spirits*, pp. 31, 32.

47. Luke 19:10.

48. 1 Timothy 4:1,2.

49. Isaiah 8:19.

50. Isaiah 8:20.

51. Exodus 20:3.

52. T.S. Eliot, "The Hollow Men," *Anthology of American Poetry* (New York: The Modern Library, 1944), p. 369.

53. Luke 24:5,6.

PART FIVE
SIGNS OF THE TIMES

"There was so much handwriting on the wall that even the wall fell down..."

Christopher Morley

CHAPTER 12

True Supernaturalism

Witches conjure spells in New York while Satan worshipers conduct marriages in San Francisco. Witch doctors practice Voodoo in New Orleans and computers arrange horoscopes in Los Angeles. Gypsies read fortune cards, ministers promote seances and seers predict California's submersion into the Pacific.

So what else is new?

Some might breathe a sigh of relief, shrug their shoulders and think, "Thank God I'm normal!" Much like the elderly Scotchman who said to his wife, "Methinks all the world is mad except me and thee, and sometimes me wonders about thee."

As we have repeatedly pointed out throughout

this book, man's preoccupation with the supernatural is nothing new—it has been going on for centuries. At times, occultism seems to fade into the woodwork, is little talked about and genders little interest. But it continues on, humming steadily in the background of history until the quiet hum crescendoes to a shriek. And again, man becomes aware of the supernatural in all its fury. Astrological charts are pulled out of drawers, crystal balls appear on tables, Satanist cults spring up overnight and the great occult phenomenon is on the rampage once again.

Several thousand years ago, the scene was not much different than today. God's chosen people, separated by Him from the pagan practices of the heathen nations around them, slowly allowed those practices to seep into their own culture and sever their supernatural fellowship with God. The prophet Jeremiah records God's anger at His people for their eagerness to follow other paths besides His. "As for your adulteries and your lustful neighings, the lewdness of your prostitution on the hills in the field, I have seen your abominations. Woe to you, O Jerusalem! How long will you remain unclean?"[1]

As a result, the Jews were taken captive and removed from their land—the land that God had given them hundreds of years before.

But God's wrath was even fiercer toward those who lured the ignorant Israelites away from Him. In a time when God had all but been forgotten by most people, a time when man was "doing his own thing" apart from God, a time when the threat of war and captivity hung ominously over the Jews, many would-be prophets were assuring the people that all would soon be well! (One is reminded of Jeane Dixon's predictions of forthcoming world peace in a world that has long since forgotten God.)

"But, 'Ah, Lord God!' I said, 'Look, the prophets are telling them, "You will not see the sword nor will you have famine, but I will give you lasting peace in this place".'

"Then the Lord said to me, 'The prophets are prophesying falsehood in My name. I have neither sent them nor commanded them nor spoken to them; they are prophesying to you a false vision, divination, futility and the deception of their own minds.'

" 'Therefore thus says the Lord concerning the prophets who are prophesying in My name, although it was not I who sent them—yet they keep saying, "There shall be no sword or famine in this land"—by sword and famine those prophets shall meet their end!'

" 'The people also to whom they are prophesying will be thrown out into the streets of Jerusalem because of the famine and the sword; and there will be no one to bury them—neither them, nor their wives, nor their sons, nor their daughters—for I shall pour out their own wickedness on them'.'"

The only supernatural activity that God encourages man to pursue is that which honestly seeks the only true God, the Father of the Lord Jesus Christ. All else—no matter how pious or pretentious it may appear—is sin before God. And God will treat it as such. (The Jews were subsequently captured and taken, from their God-given country. It was not until 1948 that the nation of Israel finally regained their promised land—a fulfillment of biblical prophecy!)

The present-day occult explosion is only symbolic of the tremendous need man has for a supernatural experience. The sincere advocate of occultism is to be commended for his knowledge that there is an unseen, supernatural world and for the zeal with which he propagates his beliefs.

This, unfortunately, is where the commendation must cease. In attempting to explain life and the meaning of the universe without accepting the authority and teaching of the Bible, the occultist assumes the role of a god by creating his own system. The alchemist deifies fire, earth, air and water; the astrologer deifies the heavens; the witch deifies talismans and charms; and the Satanist deifies himself.

God's Word and the supernatural

It is the Christian's belief that the true meaning and nature of both God and the universe is revealed to man in the Bible, written by men under the direct inspiration of God. In this Book, God has revealed the purpose of the world around us and man's role in that world. The Bible also reveals that man, in seeking to be his own god, has severed his relationship with his Creator by his own free choice. Not at all the sterile history text it is often made out to be, the Bible is the spiritual history of man since his beginnings and is alive with supernatural wisdom and insight.

Man is a "lost" creature—alienated from the life of God as well as the meaning of life. The results of this "lostness" show themselves in the current shallowness, despair and purposelessness evident in every area of culture.

The "lostness" of man throughout the world takes its toll in the denial of absolutes, the loss of values and the meaninglessness of existence. As the twentieth-century Christian philosopher and theologian Francis A. Schaeffer expresses it, man has lost his own "mannishness."³

Jesus Christ put it this way: "For what will a man be profited if he gains the whole world, and forfeits his soul?"⁴

The current interest in the supernatural is an evidence of the cry of man for something real and lasting, a faith that transcends the shallowness of a godless culture.

Dr. Martin Lloyd Jones, one of England's most recognized Christian spokesman, has well summarized the problem:

"As Christian teaching spreads, they (the satanic manifestations) almost always disappear. And this is not only true of specific Christian teaching. As long as secular teaching is ultimately based upon a background of Christianity, and is moral and good and clean and uplifting, even education and civilization seem to be able to control these evil powers, even as those Jewish exorcists were able to do.

"General education and teaching do this, and it has undoubtedly had this effect during the last one hundred years or so. But—and this is what is so important today—in an age when people no longer believe in God and begin to dabble with the unseen and to play with evil, invariably this phenomenon comes back."[3]

We live in an age of tremendous scientific advancement. Many of the old superstitions have been done away with due to a higher level of intelligence among the world's population. Yet our generation is witnessing an unbelievable resurgence of every form of occult activity.

Supernatural phenomena always rise when man's physical knowledge supersedes his moral and spiritual development.

Natural man cannot hope to understand the nature of the true supernatural world by exercising only human intelligence. There is absolutely no equation between a person's mental capacity and his spiritual insights.

The apostle Paul, in speaking of the foolishness of human wisdom, said, "But we speak God's wisdom in a mystery, the hidden wisdom, which God predestined before the ages to our glory; the wisdom which none of the rulers of this age has understood; for if they had understood it, they would not have crucified the Lord of glory."[6]

In opposition to the claims of the occult world, one must honestly and sincerely come to terms with those claims of supernatural power which are made by Jesus Christ. One cannot be a practitioner of occultism and a believer in Jesus Christ at the same time. The two are diametrically opposed. The apostle John tells us that "The Son of God appeared for this purpose, that He might destroy the works of the devil."[7] Jesus Himself refuted the Pharisees' claim that He was casting out demons by the power of Satan by claiming that one who works for Satan cannot work against Satan. It is God who opposes the devil and his works.

"He who is not with Me is against Me," Jesus said in summarizing His statement to the Pharisees.[8] And so it is today. Christ and Satan stand on opposite ends of the supernatural spectrum.

For those who believe in Jesus Christ, Satan becomes powerless to destroy. "For I am convinced," Paul wrote, "that neither death, nor life, nor angels, nor principalities, nor things present, nor things to come, nor powers, nor height, nor depth, nor any other created thing, shall be able to separate us from the love of God, which is in Christ Jesus our Lord."[9]

No philosophical system nor occult mysticism can promise such security.

Those who come to God on His terms have the right to call Him their Father. Paul states that not only can we call God Father but in the same way a child refers to his parents, we can use the simple and loving expression "papa."[10]

Not only did Jesus Christ destroy the power of sin and death over us, but He freed us to become sons of the Most High God. Rather than being our judge, God now can become our Father and we His children.

How can such a relationship come about? Very simply. It involves an honest recognition of who we really are, a true understanding of what God did through Christ's death and a sincere repentance and acknowledgment of our need for forgiveness.

Condition of man

The most blatant error into which most occultists fall is the idea that man is intrinsically good—that given enough time and opportunity he will perfect himself. The Bible clearly states that man is a sinner—both by inheritance and by choice. He inherited a sin nature in that he was born into a sinful race,[11] and he sins by choice in that he continually chooses to reject God.[12]

Only after one realizes that he is hopelessly lost and in need of a Saviour can he understand Jesus' claim that He came into the world "to seek and to save that which was lost."[13] Paul tells us that "while we were still helpless, at the right time Christ died for the ungodly."[14] And again, he says, "God demonstrates His own love towards us, in that while we were yet sinners, Christ died for us."[15]

In sending His own Son to be the final sacrifice for our sin, God amply demonstrated His eternal love for mankind. "He Himself is the propitiation (satisfaction) for our sins; and not for ours only, but also for those of the whole world.[16] He (God) made Him who knew no sin (Christ) to be sin on our behalf, that we might become the righteousness of God in Him (Christ)."[17]

Recognition of this should lead one to "repentance toward God and faith in our Lord Jesus Christ."[18] In repentance, man turns from his sin. In faith, he entrusts his life to the keeping power of God. When a person places complete faith and trust in Jesus Christ, he receives total forgiveness of his sins—past, present and future. "I will forgive their iniquity, and their sin I will remember no more,"[19] God promises those who trust Him. The slate is not only wiped clean but thrown away and man is finally freed from the accusations of a guilty conscience before God.

This is the uniqueness of the Christian faith. Any person, irregardless of age, race or intellect, can experience the new birth into the life of Jesus Christ. "If any man is in Christ, he is a new creature; the old things passed away; behold, new things have come."[20]

With such a supernatural faith, man need no longer be afraid of "the other side." This promise is given to every true believer: "For God has not given us a spirit of timidity, but of power and love and discipline."[21]

Equipped with a true understanding of the supernatural world, the Christian can face not only life but also death with real peace. It is written of the great Christian evangelist, Dwight L. Moody, concerning his grandchildren who had died sometime before, that upon his deathbed he looked up and cried in triumph—"Dwight! Irene! I can see the children's faces!" Such is the joy of the believer. Even as the apostle Paul exclaimed, "Oh death, where is your victory? Oh death, where is your sting?"[22]

The true believer looks forward to that day in the not-too-distant future when it shall be fulfilled that "the God of peace will soon crush Satan under your feet."[23]

But for the person who has not put his trust in Jesus Christ as Saviour and Lord, the future holds only the promise of eternal separation from an all-loving yet all-righteous God. Being a God of holiness and justice, He cannot as much as look upon sin, much less accept the one who refuses His gift of eternal life. "He who has the Son has life; he who does not have the Son of God does not have the life."[24]

No seance, no hexagram, no Ouija board no crystal ball, no "fortune-teller" can match His guarantee of eternal life or His promise of divine peace.

Jesus said, "But no one can enter the strong man's house and plunder his property unless he first binds the strong man, and then he will plunder his house."[25] The world is Satan's fortress, but Jesus has broken into the strong one's castle and deprived him of his prey.

God presents to us today the same alternatives that He presented the children of Israel centuries ago, "I call heaven and earth to witness against you today, that I have set before you life and death, . . . *So choose life . . .*"[26]

Footnotes for Chapter 12

1. Jeremiah 13:27.
2. Jeremiah 14:13-16.
3. For further study: Francis A. Schaeffer, *The God Who Is There* (1968) and H.R. Rookmaaker, *Modern Art and the Death of a Culture* (1970), published by Inter Varsity Press, Downers Grove, Illinois.
4. Matthew 16:26.
5. Martin Lloyd Jones, *The Westminster Record*, vol. 36, no. 11, November, 1962.
6. 1 Corinthians 2:7,8.
7. 1 John 3:8.
8. Matthew 12:30.
9. Romans 8:38,39.
10. Romans 8:15.
11. Romans 5:12-14.
12. Romans 3:23; Ecclesiastes 7:20.
13. Luke 19:10; Matthew 18:11.
14. Romans 5:6.
15. Romans 5:8.
16. 1 John 2:2.
17. 2 Corinthians 5:21.
18. Acts 20:21.
19. Jeremiah 31:34.
20. 2 Corinthians 5:17.
21. 2 Timothy 1:7.
22. 1 Corinthians 15:55.
23. Romans 16:20.
24. 1 John 5:12.
25. Mark 3:27.
26. Deuteronomy 30:19.

A Definition of Terms

ALCHEMY   The ancient art of analysis and prediction through the basic elements of the universe: fire, earth, air and water.

AMULET   A charm said to possess certain "powers" for good or evil—worn as jewelry and used in magic ritual.

ANGELS   Spiritual beings created by God to worship Him. Some assigned to protect those who believe in the true God. ("Bad angels" or "demons" are those self-willed spirits who have rebelled against almighty God to serve the "Prince of Darkness," Satan.)

APPARITION   The materialization of a spirit being or an illusion created by same.

APPORTS   The phenomena of objects being fetched over great distances and through solid walls by the exercise of para-natural mental powers.

BLACK MAGIC   The religion of Satan-worship. The devil is given equal standing with God and worshiped through hideous ritual and sacrifice (animal and human).

BLACK MASS   The Satanic antithesis of the Roman Catholic Mass. Often accompanied by animal or human sacrifice, the mass is a perverted ritual of sacrilege. The communion wafer (host) and wine are spit upon or sexually defiled—all references to God and Christ are omitted or desecrated—hymns are sung backwards—crosses inverted, etc.

BLOOD PACT (with the devil)   An agreement with Satan whereby the person agrees to give his soul in exchange for temporary worldly benefits. Such agreements are always signed in blood.

CABALA   The "hidden wisdom" claimed by cabalists to have been given to Abraham by God and handed down over generations. Its basic concept involves the theory of the soul's descent and ascent through 10 "spheres" to ultimate union with God.

CLAIRVOYANT   A person with extrasensory telepathic powers who can discern things not seen or known by the five senses.

CONTROL SPIRIT   The spirit which makes contact between the medium and another spirit from "the other side" during spiritualist seances. The contact spirit is usually named and reappears to one particular medium throughout his life.

COVEN   "Brotherhood" or "congregation." An assembly of 13 or less witches. Led by the Head Witch, today's coven is similar to a private religious "order."

DEMON   A created spirit being. One of the angels that rebelled against God prior to the creation of the world (i.e., "evil spirit").

DOWSER (DAUSER)   One who searches for lost, hidden, or uncovered objects with the use of a "divining rod" (a long stick or pole with a V-shaped handle).

ESBATH   The witchcraft celebration in parks or forests during the nights of the full moon; nude participants play games and follow ceremonial rituals akin to the Old Religion of Diana-worship.

ESP   Abbreviation for "extrasensory perception" (i.e., "mental telepathy").

EXORCISM The process whereby a person is freed from demonic control ("demon possession") by supernatural power.

FAMILIAR SPIRIT Term used by spiritualists to designate the spirit of the deceased which manifests itself at a seance. This is actually an evil spirit which impersonates the deceased (i.e., a spirit "familiar" with the dead person).

HEX A spell or evil wish cast upon another person. Hexing usually involves the invocation of demonic powers.

HEXAGRAM A pentagram with one ray of the star pointing upwards; used as a religious symbol in witchcraft.

HOROSCOPE (Greek, "hour-watcher") A diagram of the position of the stars and planets at the time of one's birth. Thought by astrologers to reveal an individual's personality and destiny as well as predict national events.

INCANTATION A chant or song used in pagan rituals to invoke the blessing or curse of the gods.

LEVITATION The floating-in-air of a person or object. More often than not the work of a professional trickster.

MATERIALIZATION The form in which a spirit being makes itself visible to human beings. Usually recognizable as the likeness of a deceased individual.

MEDIUM A person (male or female) used as a relay station between the seen and the unseen world. A professional who can lapse into trance at any given time; often has a keen sense of ESP.

MENTAL TELEPATHY The ability to send and receive thought transferences. Conscious as well as unconscious thoughts can be transmitted to another person without the use of the five senses.

NECROMANCY Fortune-telling by the use of the dead. In its widest sense, it could include seances—usually thought of in conjunction with Voodoo.

OCCULT That which is "hidden" or "secret"; always has to do with the spiritual, unseen world.

OUIJA BOARD An ancient device for discerning the will of the spirits. A flat wooden board with each letter of the alphabet as well as ancient symbols and a "yes" and "no" area. Seekers place fingertips on a triangle which often moves out of control in spelling out its message.

221

PALMISTRY The art of predicting one's future through careful study of his hand. (Origin in Greek mythology where an infant grasped his mother's umbilical cord at birth in order to prevent his fall—thereby causing lines in his palm.)

PENTAGRAM A five-pointed star used as a religious symbol: always pointing up in witchcraft rituals and down in Black Magic ceremonies. In Black Magic, the head of a goat is usually found in the center with two horns pointed defiantly toward heaven and three pointed downward representing the Trinity denied.

POLTERGEISTS Noisy and often visible manifestations of the spirit world; usually thought of in conjunction with haunted houses (i.e., "ghosts").

PRECOGNITION Awareness of an event before it happens. (Most often involves personal tragedies and deaths.)

PSYCHIC A person with certain sensitivity to mental telepathy, precognition and prophecy.

SATANISM Devil-worship (i.e., "Black Magic").

SEANCE Meeting at which communication with the "other side" is attempted through a medium; usually held around a circular table in a dimly-lit room.

SEER A fortune-teller; usually designates one who uses crystal balls, cards, etc. (i.e., "soothsayer").

SOOTHSAYER Obsolete for "forunte-teller"; one who predicts future events, both national and personal.

SOUL-TRAVEL The idea that a person's soul may leave his body, observe and relay incidents and happenings hundreds of miles away. Most "soul travel" is merely a keen sense of ESP.

SPIRIT WRITING Writing done unconsciously by a medium while in a trance. Oftentimes results in a weird arrangement of words and phrases resembling an undeciphered "code." (Spirit Painting, another trance phenomenon, is done in similar fashion.)

TELEKINESIS The movement or rearrangement of objects by spirit beings. True table-lifting and other physical phenomena are examples.

TRANCE A state of semiconsciousness into which a genuine medium lapses during a seance; at such times, the mind is made void of any conscious thought and becomes a vehicle for spirit communication.

VOODOO   Ancient African ancestor-worship from the West Indies. National religion of Haiti with offshoots in the States.

WARLOCK   A devotee of witchcraft; one who practices magic ritual (ancient: a male witch).

WITCHES' SABBATH (SABBAT)   The four main holidays of the witchcraft religion: May Eve, Lammas, Halloween (or All Hallows Eve), and Candlemas (or Brigid's Day).

ZODIAC   The division of the heavens into twelve sections ("houses") each with a title appropriate to the star formations ("signs") in that house. Each "house" is thought to affect human experience.